P9-EAO-763

How to Escape
Lifetime
Security and
Pursue Your
Impossible Dream

A Guide to Transforming Your Career

Kenneth Atchity

HELIOS PRESS
NEW YORK

B

650.14
ATC

© 2004 by Kenneth Atchity.

08   07   06   05   04   5   4   3   2   1

Published by Helios Press
An imprint of Allworth Communications, Inc.
10 East 23rd Street, New York, NY 10010

Typography by Integra Software Services
Page composition by SR Desktop Services, Ridge, NY
Cover photography by Photolibrary.com/Photonica
Cover design by Derek Bacchus

LIBRARY OF CONGRESS CATALOGING-IN-PUBLICATION DATA

Atchity, Kenneth John.
    How to escape lifetime security and pursue your impossible
    dream: a guide to changing your career/by Kenneth Atchity.
        p. cm.
    ISBN 1-58115-385-6
    1. Career changes.   2. Vocational guidance.   3. Job
    satisfaction.   I. Title.

    HF5384.A837 2004
    650.14—dc22
                                                2004012597
Printed in Canada

Though this be madness, yet there is method in it.
—Shakespeare, *Hamlet*

The difference between myself and a mad man
Is that I am not mad.—Salvador Dali

Dream abides. It is the only thing that abides. Vision abides.
—Miguel de Unamuno

I used to think people doing things weird were weird. That was
before I realized that people doing things weird weren't weird
at all. It was the people who were saying they were weird who
were weird.—Paul McCartney

I think the only immoral thing is for a being not to live every
moment of his life with the utmost intensity.
—José Ortega y Gasset

ALSO BY KENNETH ATCHITY

In Praise of Love
Eterne in Mutabilitie: The Unity of *The Faerie Queene*
Homer's *Iliad*: The Shield of Memory
Sleeping with an Elephant: Selected Poems
Italian Literature: Roots & Branches
A Writer's Time: A Guide to the Creative Process, from Vision
    through Revision
Homer: Critical Essays
The Mercury Transition
Cajun Household Wisdom
The Renaissance Reader
Writing Treatments That Sell
The Classical Greek Reader
The Classical Roman Reader
How to Publish Your Novel

For Kayoko
"for the duration"

contents

acknowledgments

Writing this book was a constant reminder of the people in my life who taught me about creativity, and of my own supportive inner circle that inspired, protected, and encouraged me during my own career transition. I've been fortunate to have had sterling mentors, and a small but fiercely loyal band of supporters: You know who you are, and that I'm grateful for your being my creative family.

I'm most appreciative of my agents Sasha Goodman, Denise Marcil, and Sandra Watt, as well as of Barbara Sher and Marsha Sinetar for encouraging me to write the book of which this is a revision, *The Mercury Transition: How to Escape from Lifetime Security to Follow Your Impossible Dream* (Longmeadow, 1994), and that book's editors, Pam Liflander and Jo Glorie. My clients and students have been a constant source of ideas and responses, especially Steve Alten, David Batstone, Shirley Palmer, John Robert Marlow, James Michael Pratt, Cheryl and Haim Saban, Micheal S. Simpson, Judy Cairo, and Governor Jesse Ventura. And to my able associates at Atchity Entertainment International, Inc., a huge thank-you for your hard work and faith—especially David and Joanna Angsten, Brenna Lui, Mike Kuciak, Margaret O'Connor; and for editing this version, Andrea McKeown and Julie Mooney.

Most of all, for sharing in the struggle, egging me on, and just plain tolerating the pressures I put them and myself under, my loving thanks go to my partners Chi-Li Wong, John Scott Shepherd, Sue Baechler, and Garby Leon; to Mike Braverman,

David Foster, Matt Gross, King Grossman, Craig Perry, Darryl Porter, Richard Rappaport, Richard Rosenthal, and Warren Zide Dennis Stanfill; my son Vincent and his wife Kris Puopolo, and my daughter Rosemary and her husband John McKenna; and David Adashek. And to the memory of my father, Frederick Atchity, the Accountant, and my mother, Myrza Marie Atchity, the wild-eyed Visionary—now forever presiding within.

Finally, I owe a measureless debt of gratitude to Kayoko Mitsumatsu, my New Year's wife and the woman of my dreams, who had to wait to appear in my life until I got my act together—and, on a daily basis, makes sure I keep it that way.

Los Angeles and New York

1

"go for it!"

jung: Neurosis is no substitute for genuine suffering.
atchity: Take pride in your pain.

How many times have you felt as if you were hurtling toward a brick wall at ninety mph and someone supposedly dear to you gave you the advice, "Slow down!" or "Relax"? As many times as I've been advised to slow down, I've wondered whether hitting the wall at thirty mph was truly preferable to hitting it at ninety. If you're going to go splat, make it a complete splat! How else will you find out in time whether that wall is, in fact, as you imagined, the secret door to your dreams?

This book is about the speed and shape of your creative life— and about the wall that so often becomes a door. Your chosen speed and trajectory are precisely what distinguish you, a Type C personality, from the others who are saying, "Relax."

If you're one of those fortunate souls whose attitude is always perfect, who goes through life with an eternal smile of confidence, and who has never found it necessary to scream or cry, this book is not for you. I wish I could say, through the years of my midlife career transit, that I've always been "up." The truth is, I've had to build my "upness," sometimes from what felt like scratch, nearly every day. I like to think it's because the life I've chosen requires me to do things I've never done before, things I'm not always certain I can find a way of doing.

"what makes you an authority?"

einstein: The punishment fate has given me for my hatred of authority is making me one.

atchity: Authority comes from describing the clear pattern things reveal in retrospect.

Once upon a time I resigned my position as tenured professor of comparative literature at Occidental College in Los Angeles to pursue a new, full-time career as freelance writer, independent producer, literary manager, and entrepreneurial "story merchant." I exchanged a thirty-year "comfort horizon" (how much of the future you can envision as being covered by income-generating contracts presently in hand) for one that has ranged from a mere twenty-four hours to twelve months at the very best—normally hovering precariously between forty-five and ninety days. When people told me that my midlife career change was insane, I reminded them (and myself) of Salvador Dali's taunt: "The only difference between myself and a madman is that I am not mad." Regardless of how that struck my interrogator, it made *me* feel better.

My decision to resign from my tenured position became final in the middle of a December snowstorm in Montreal, where I was taking a leave of absence from Occidental College to supervise the production of the *Shades of Love* series of romantic comedies, which I had conceived and was producing for Lorimar-Warner-Astral. The decision followed on the heels of an event that brought the familiar sensation that everything happens for a reason: I was scheduled to play the extra part of a professor in Mort Ransen's *Sincerely, Violet*, but had been delayed by a snowstorm. By the time I finally arrived on the set, the scene had already been shot, using an extra. I decided right then and there that I simply wasn't meant to play a professor, even in fiction—that it was high time to resign my tenure. My appearance as an extra was rescheduled for the next day: I ended up playing a graphologist.

Although the incident in Montreal provoked immediate action, the decision had been a long time in the making, first conceived twelve years earlier while I was serving as a Fulbright professor at the University of Bologna. On Valentine's Day of that year, I received a telegram from Occidental's dean of the faculty informing me that I'd been granted tenure.

My immediate reaction to this news surprised me: I became depressed.

The depression continued for at least a year, compounded by my difficulty finding colleagues who could relate to such a bizarre reaction to what everyone else considered good news. I should have been ecstatic.

I finally figured it out for myself: I felt trapped, suffocated. My oldest recurrent nightmare as a child was of being suffocated by an enormous blanket not of my own weaving. Yes, the box I now found myself in was a comfortable one; but it was still a box—a gilded cage. As much as I loved teaching, as much as I had suc-ceeded at it, I was having trouble with the thought that for the next thirty-nine years I'd be able to predict my schedule twelve months in advance. I felt that my life was spinning out of control, coming to an end, and that without knowing how, I had prema-turely become a zombie.

I knew I had to escape.

I also knew I had something to contrast these dark feelings with, something that seemed trivial at the time. Even as a professor I couldn't keep my fingers out of various business pies. I ran a con-sulting company that specialized in helping writers perfect their work, translated business documents from and into several lan-guages, and published and distributed poetry quarterlies. One day I received a most unexpected call out of the blue—from the State

Department in Washington. A Yemeni diplomat was in the United States, wanting to meet with an American businessman and professor who was also a poet. It scares me to think how they found me, but they asked if I'd be willing to spend an afternoon with him.

He flew to Los Angeles and picked me up at my consulting office in Glendale. We spent a delightful afternoon talking about poetry, business, literature, and world affairs and were mutually impressed at the other's diverse interests. Early in the conversation, he'd asked about my origins, and I'd explained my Lebanese/French Louisiana ancestry. He told me that I was following in the traditions of the Lebanese—Phoenicians originally—by being an educated "story merchant," who believed enough in the poems and short stories I read and wrote to publish them. He pointed out that writing and publishing your own poetry, and that of others, was respectable behavior, and I couldn't help but think of the president of my college who'd once asked, "What other entrepreneurial activities are you engaged in?" when he received a complaint from a fellow faculty member that I was distributing literary magazines. The word "entrepreneurial" sounded like "mud-dredging" in his Ivy-League drawl.

At Occidental I'd created internships that allowed students to work at film studios, newspapers, and publishing companies in the real world. As I lectured on creativity and writing on campuses throughout the country I began feeling more and more dishonest about the secure life I'd chosen for myself.

I also realized two things: I realized I hadn't really chosen to be a professor. I'd simply responded to job offers after finishing graduate school, accepting the most attractive one in a place that was most conducive to raising my young family. At the time, I also imagined that being a professor meant teaching all the time, without foreseeing the realities of committees, bureaucratic red tape, tenure battles that destroyed lives, and the ceaseless futility of campus politics.

And just how safe *was* the academic profession anyway? While tenure seemed like a magical word for some people, I calculated that the economic realities were such that even tenure would not be immune should the college find itself in dire financial straits. The safety my colleagues valued so highly was, I concluded, merely an illusion of security. I'd also never been comfortable in a costume, except maybe on Halloween. And being a professor, complete with tweed jackets with leather elbow pads, was costume. The word "uniform" was too painful to contemplate.

At the same time I realized that I preferred the illusion of freedom to the illusion of security. When I talked about my restlessness with novelist John Gardner, who at the time was editing my first book on Homer, he told me I was crazy; that I should remain a professor and do whatever else I wanted to do from that secure foundation. As a creative entrepreneur himself, he very wisely couldn't recommend his lifestyle when he compared it to mine.

So I hung on another year or so, satisfying my restlessness by founding and editing off-campus magazines: *CQ: Poetry and Art*; the interdisciplinary journal *DreamWorks* (dedicated to the study of dreams and the arts), with my colleague Marsha Kinder; and a Pasadena arts newspaper, *Follies*.

Then I had the good fortune to meet a man whose columns in the *Saturday Review* I'd enjoyed as a teenager, Norman Cousins. No doubt reflecting the mood I was in that year, I found myself offering a course titled "Literature and Death"; and, inspired by reading Norman's *Anatomy of an Illness*, invited him as a guest speaker. He accepted. During his presentation to my class, Norman used Ortega y Gasset's observation about intensity, quoted on the dedication page of this book: "I think the only immoral thing is for a being not to live every moment of his life with the utmost intensity."

Never having heard anyone else but myself cite these stirring words, I was stunned.

After class, I asked him to stop by my office for a minute on our way to the Faculty Club for lunch. I wanted to show Norman the plaque hanging above my desk, bearing the very words he'd quoted. He was touched. En route to lunch, I asked him if I could impose on a few moments of his time, at his convenience, to talk with him about "what I want to do when I grow up." He laughed, and asked me if I played tennis.

A few days later, to my pleasure and surprise, he called to ask if I could be the fourth in a doubles game. After a rousing set at Bea Arthur's house in Mandeville Canyon, Norman listened to my achievements, dreams, and ambitions, and then offered me his advice.

"Whatever you do," he told me, "don't ever give up your diversity."

I couldn't believe my ears. All my previous advisers had consistently said the opposite. When I had first proposed the idea for *DreamWorks* to Paul Chance at *Psychology Today*, he'd responded with a long, thoughtful letter, criticizing the magazine's diversity, closing it with the words, "Find your niche, young man, find your niche." We proceeded with *DreamWorks* anyway, and it went on to win awards for its interdisciplinary focus.

All my life I'd been seeking my niche among niches defined by others. Norman was advising me to create my own Type C niche, defining it with sufficient diversity to replace the suffocation response with excitement and hope.

His second suggestion threw me for even more of a loop. He told me that, in his opinion, the best place to exercise my particular talents and ambitions was the entertainment industry. When I replied that I knew nothing about that world, he recommended that I read William Goldman's *Adventures in the Screen Trade* (Goldman's scripts and novels include *Marathon Man, Butch Cassidy and the Sundance Kid*, and *Magic*). I was ready to follow Norman's advice when, part way through Goldman's book, I encountered what the screenwriter-novelist called the "single most important fact" of the entire movie business: "Nobody knows anything." I realized immediately that I was on a level playing field, and that I'd found my second career.

By the time I'd finished Goldman's book, I was convinced that I shouldn't go into my new career solely as a writer. For one

thing, it would limit my ability to express other talents, like sales-
manship, management, and entrepreneurial instincts. For another,
writers have little leverage in this great big bad world until
they're established. Unless they're lucky, they could wait forever to
be recognized. I didn't want to rely on luck, and I didn't have forever. I realized that I needed to learn enough about the industry
to become a producer, having little idea then about what a producer does. At that point, serendipity again came to my assistance
in the person of A. John Graves, who happened to be enrolled in
my graduate course at California State College, Los Angeles, on
"Shakespeare's Ten Worst Plays."

Formerly an executive at NBC, John was now working as
an independent producer. He approached me after class one
night and asked if I'd ever considered a career in show business.
I couldn't believe my ears. A few lunches later, I had the mentor
I needed—and a desk full of contracts to read. (My theory was
that learning a new business would go faster if I started with the
endpoint of a deal.) I read every contract I could get my hands
on. I'll never forget one that included, "Accounting terms shall be
defined in such fashion as the Twentieth Century Fox accounting
department shall define them at such time, if any, that litigation is
entered into among the parties." Although I would wrestle with
the concept many times in the future, I had just encountered for
the first time what's known in the Biz as "creative accounting."

Four years later, just after the *New York Times* had printed
a full-page story about my Lorimar-Warner-Astral series of
romantic comedies, I bumped into a mentor from my former
life, Bart Giamatti, in the elevator of the New York City Yale
Club.

"Atchity," he said, "what's this I hear about a professor of comparative literature producing romance movies?"

"What's this I hear about the president of Yale becoming the
baseball commissioner?"

"Touché," he laughed.

Apparently, I hadn't fallen too far from the tree.

In making the move from security to freedom, substituting an illusion I preferred for an illusion that was suffocating me, I had entered a full-blown midlife crisis. If I'd taken the ten-question stress test two years after my resignation from Occidental, I would have set the record for major life changes.

Within three years, I'd changed jobs, homes, cities, spouse. And my father died.

In the midst of one particular crisis in my brilliant new career, I found myself in San Francisco, at the home of dream therapist Gayle Delaney (*Living Your Dreams*). Gayle suggested that I incubate a dream to determine whether I truly thought I had within me the resources to continue along the course I'd set for myself.

That night I dreamed that I found myself between two apparently equal serpents, and realized they were in the process of devouring me. But they didn't. I woke up elated.

"What do you think the serpents represent?" Gayle asked the next morning.

"My problems? My conflicting motivations?" I thought about it, deciding that they must relate to my theory of the two parts of the mind being in constant war with each other. By the time we'd worked it out, I realized that the dream was directly related to my lifelong fascination, as a student and teacher of mythology, with Mercury's caduceus—the flowering rod, plume, and serpents (although some representations show only one serpent, I've always favored the ones with two).

The snakes in my dream were the Past and the Future, with my own personal skills between them in the Present, barely managing to keep me upright. The Past was trying to pull me back; the Future, with all its fears and anxieties, was trying to devour my energy. But I was safe in the Present because the focal point of safety lies in the centered self that has learned, by mastering itself, to master the world.

As a student of Homer's *Odyssey*, I recognized that the mythic origins of the dream were related to the Greek concept of *techné*, the protean virtue of Athene and Hermes (Mercury), whose mortal counterpart is Homer's hero Odysseus. As Odysseus was able to vanquish the serpentine monsters encountered on his embattled journey to Ithaka, I would be able to master the draconian serpents threatening me from both sides.

The dream was reminding me, in other words, that fighting dragons was my natural strength. No wonder, despite my high anxiety, I was essentially content with my decision. My contentment had reached its height one blizzardy day on a flight between Montreal and Toronto, when the prospect of the plane going down in the storm didn't concern me enough to make me look up from the script I was editing. At the time, we were still shooting one film in Montreal; but we were already in postproduction on another film at Pathé's sound lab in Toronto. A final mix (where the music is added to the film's sound effects) was scheduled that night. Everyone thought I should skip the mix because of the weather, but I was determined to master every detail of my new career, so I went to Dorval Airport. Once there, I discovered that Air Canada had canceled its flight to Toronto because of the storm. But a smaller, prop-driven airliner was scheduled to leave in ten minutes. I decided to take it, ignoring the fear of flying I'd always previously experienced.

As the plane lumbered through the snowstorm, it occurred to me that the possibility that I might die on this flight didn't disturb me. I was living my dream, and dying in the middle of my dream would be a happy death. In her studies of death and the dying, Elizabeth Kübler-Ross found that people "are not afraid of death per se, but of the incompleteness of their lives, of dying prematurely."

Up there in the blizzard, on that plane, I felt that my life was complete. And I realized that I'd have to expand my dream to give myself a reason to continue living with this wonderful sense of fulfillment.

I began to accept that my view of success wasn't about garnering achievements as much as about achieving (in the words of Robert Browning, "Ah, but a man's reach should exceed his grasp,/Or what's a heaven for?"); and that this view made me different from many of the people who, along the way, came to me for jobs, consultations, or conversations about how to do what I had done. Listening to them, consulting with them, I realized that it was product, not process, that turned them on. I began to see that whether they are salespeople or athletes, writers or inventors, builders, proprietors of boutiques, or entrepreneurs, Type C personalities are quite different from others. They're in love with the phrase, "Go for it."

People tell me that it took a lot of courage to give up the total security of a tenured position. The comment sounded alien to me at first, then started to trouble me more and more. I've always taken pride in doing something good, and "courage" sounds very good. At one point early in my new career, at Marsha Sinetar's suggestion, Dr. Joyce Brothers and her television crew came to interview me about career change. As usual, I was under enormous pressure, but I did my best to talk sensibly about why I had made my own transition and what it felt like to be in the middle of it. Dr. Joyce kept saying it was "courageous," and I kept changing the subject to my worries about the wolf at the door. But when the program aired a few months later, I had to admit that even I was impressed with how my story sounded. One of my fellow interviewees was a hairdresser who'd gone after her medical degree in psychiatry at the age of fortysomething. Earning that credential had allowed her to exchange listening to clients for $25 an hour to listening to them for $125 an hour. Another was a man in his eighties, who was just receiving his law degree—his fifth career change. He recounted his experience on registration day:

"The young man behind me in line finally asked, 'Sir, may I ask you what you're doing in this line?'"

"What line should I be in?" the octogenarian had answered.

I could see now why what I had done sounded courageous to others. But I didn't feel courageous. Instead, on many mornings and afternoons, and especially evenings, when I had absolutely no idea how I could continue for another hour, I felt certain I'd made a gigantic mistake. Had I foreseen what it would cost me in every aspect of my life, I told myself, I might never have undertaken my new career. Visualizing the future is one thing. Seeing it in actuality would have discouraged me.

Instead of courage, the word I came to use was "challenge." I needed to feel challenged, needed to challenge myself. My career transit was a necessity, not a luxury, keeping my sense of self intact. Did I have the strength and stamina to face the unfamiliar adversities I had chosen for myself? And to be called, in the process, "self-centered," "selfish," "irresponsible," and "crazy"?

sophocles: It's a terrible thing to look upon your troubles and to realize that you yourself and no one else are responsible for them.

atchity: It's a wonderful thing to look upon the challenges you've created for yourself and to embrace them as your own.

Let's admit that it takes courage to express your Type C personality—to live with the consequences of your decision to be yourself, whatever you conceive that self to be. It takes courage to stand apart from all the "normal" people out there who criticize and raise their eyebrows, wondering why you're so crazy (while they wonder, to themselves, why they can't be a little more like you).

Even more, it takes courage to stand against the enemy within: the normal person inside you, shaped by your parents and the Society of the Non-weird, who spends his every waking effort trying to stop you from doing something as insane as quitting a high-paying, secure position to pursue your idiosyncratic need for freedom, creativity, and self-definition.

Career transition isn't recommended for the overly critical or for those who need security. It's for those who know that the ultimate challenge lies in the self-knowledge that comes only when you pit skills beyond your present imagining against the relentless resourcefulness of a world of troubles.

Theodore Roosevelt was such a man:

> It is not the critic who counts, not the man who points
> out how the strong man stumbled, or where the doer of
> deeds could have done them better. The credit belongs to
> the man who is actually in the arena; whose face is marred
> by dust and sweat and blood; who strives valiantly; who
> errs and comes up short again and again; who knows the
> great enthusiasms; the great devotions; and spends himself
> in a worthy cause; who, at the best, knows in the end the
> triumph of high achievement; and who, at the worst, if he
> fails, at least fails while daring greatly, so that his place shall
> never be with those cold and timid souls who know nei-
> ther victory nor defeat.

Roosevelt makes risk taking and being creative sound glamorous
to those who haven't gone for it. He, like those who have gone
for their dreams, knew better. No one in his right mind would
encourage anyone over the age of twenty-five to sacrifice security
for the uncharted territory of a new career—unless the seeker
came up with the idea himself.

But if you feel a strong need to change, if you're one of those
people who long to live the creative life of a professional writer,
this book might help you chart that new territory. Francisco de
Goya complained, "The sleep of reason produces monsters." This
book may help you deal with the monsters of your imagination
and the undiscovered country down the road not previously
taken.

The ultimate investment is investing in yourself, by designing
a life around your unique interests. Everyone might tell you that
this is the way to happiness, but very few people will encourage
you to pursue such selfishness. Even fewer pursue it for themselves. Those who do are the ones who make a difference. When
creative career change is successful, it leads to fulfillment. But what
about when it's not successful? As you get into it, you quickly

begin to realize that success is ephemeral. Not simply because change is tough, but because even the word "success" must be redefined in order to continue being useful. I didn't feel successful after having produced my first films, but I felt very successful *while* producing them.

Aside from suffocation, my greatest fear in life had always been that I would come to feel that my energies weren't being challenged, that my time on earth was being wasted. I'd reacted strongly to the poignancy of former President Lyndon Johnson's telltale comment: "To hunger for use, and to go unused, that is the greatest hunger of all." The person who engages in career transition has made the conscious decision to respond to the need to be used and useful, to follow in the footsteps of George Bernard Shaw, who wrote forty-one of his fifty-two produced plays after age forty-five, *Pygmalion* at age fifty-seven, *Saint Joan* at age sixty-seven, and *Buoyant Billions* at age ninety-one. Shaw wrote:

> This is the true joy in life, the being used for a purpose recognized by yourself as a mighty one; the being thoroughly worn out before you are thrown on the scrap heap; the being a force of Nature instead of a feverish selfish little clod of ailments and grievances complaining that the world will not devote itself to making you happy.

Everyone's first career is an accident. Your next career, the child of your choice, is your mighty purpose that makes life worth living.

2

our maddening type c personality

dad: No risk.
mom: Go for it!
oracle of delphi: Get to know thyself.
atchity: One at a time, please. One at a time.

My father, bless his soul, was probably the classic Type A personality—a workaholic accountant whose favorite evening pastime was to disappear into his downstairs office to work on his books. No one ever heard him say he loved accounting. As far as he was concerned, accounting was simply what he had to do, and the more he did it, the more money he made. As he worked his way through life, he kept postponing the gratification that others were urging upon him: trips to Europe, automobile trips across the country, a shopping spree to buy things his hard work had entitled him to. He was a child of the Depression and of an entrepreneurial immigrant father to whom bankruptcy was no stranger. Attaining the American dream was my grandfather's primary motivation. Holding on to it—security—was my father's. Even when security was no longer an issue, Dad continued to work as though it were. Sadly, that work was simply a means to an end, and until mere months before the end of his life, he rarely took time to enjoy the end his means had earned him.

My mother, on the other hand, was always urging him, and her children, to take risks. She'd come a long way from the ten-acre farm in French Louisiana where she was born—through nursing school in New Orleans, and to my father's family's hometown of Kansas City, Missouri. She saw all her children through high school and some through college and graduate school. "If he can do it," she would tell us, referring to a headline or TV bulletin about someone's achievement, "you can do it too. Just do it." She once helped my brother sell the most Little League baseball tickets on his team by insisting that he cover every floor in all the sky-scrapers in downtown Kansas City. He was exhausted, but he won. No one even came close.

When my father died, I sat at the desk in his den staring at a wooden-block slogan that had been enshrined next to his pen set for as long as I could remember: RISK NOTHING, LOSE NOTHING. For the first time I realized that, to him, the slogan meant, *Don't take the risk.* All my life, I'd read it as, *Risk it!* Only at his death did I understand exactly how much his perspective had differed from mine.

w. s. merwin: The story of the hinge is that it is dreaming to fly. "No hinge has ever flown," the locks tell it again and again. "That is why we are dreaming," it answers, "and then we will teach the doors."

I like to think it's because of the inner pull between my Accountant father and my Visionary mother that I ended up with what I call, for the sake of shorthand, a Type C personality: C for creative, C for Mercury's caduceus (that magic wand), and, yes, C for crazy. Like the Type A, described by Drs. Meyer Friedman and Ray Rosenman in their classic *Type A Behavior and Your Heart*, the Type C is hard-driving and highly time-conscious, and seeks out increasing levels of stress.

But there's a crucial difference between the Type C and the traditional, overstressed, and intrinsically unhappy Type A, one largely based on a higher degree of awareness. The philosopher José Ortega y Gasset defines a hero as "one who wants to be himself." In this sense, the Type C is heroic, insisting on choosing only stress that brings him pleasure, the stress brought on by pursuing his impossible dream; and also on taking responsibility for his choice. As a result, then, once they "get their heads together," and learn to relax (like the Type B), Type Cs thrive on the very stress that grinds away at the Type A.

At its most functional, the Type C personality is the creative personality, obsessed with making visionary dreams come true; and, almost always, whether happily or not, paying a price for it on an hourly basis. An old Cajun saying puts it this way: "You have two choices: Forget your dreams, or pay for them." The Type C has figured out that we only live once, as far as we know for sure. The risk of feeling that we haven't fully lived our lives, haven't explored our fullest potential, is a far greater risk than any risk we might face by pursuing a dream that, arguably, might be considered by some insane.

If you're the classic Type A personality, you're an overachiever, a workaholic who's considered overly stressed and in danger of heart attack because you can't stop working, yet you don't particularly love your work. If you're a Type C personality, like most of the writers, directors, and artistic entrepreneurs I consult or partner with and/or manage, you're stressed primarily because the work you love is on the cutting edge, and is therefore misunderstood and rejected most of the time, leaving you feeling misunderstood and anxious as a result. The Type C embraces Sigmund Freud's conclusion (without necessarily embracing Sigmund Freud!) that the two aims in life that most lead to fulfillment are "to work and to love."

At his least functional, the Type C lives up to the reputation he has with others who identify C with "crazy." A number of recent studies suggest a direct link between mental illness and creativity.

Maybe it was easy enough for Salvador Dali ("The difference between myself and a madman is that I am not mad") to distinguish between himself and a madman, but the early-career Type C isn't always so self-confident. Though the Type C is compelled to give up the risk-free path of security to pursue the rocky road of his dreams, he's very often unsure of himself as he starts along that road, even when he seems to be succeeding. As other recent studies have pointed out, the Type C considers himself an impostor in the very world he's creating.

With this tenuous distinction between creativity and craziness, nothing is more important to the Type C than taking care of his head. Which means finding the key to understanding what's going on inside it: which of those voices I'm hearing are sane, which are insane, which are right and which are wrong, which come from my dream and which come from what others would have me do—which to listen to, which to silence at any given moment. The stakes in this self-understanding, the very foundation of self-investment, couldn't be higher. What makes some people wear their creativity lightly, to a natural joyous end (Pablo Picasso, Thomas Edison, Henry Ford, Audrey Hepburn), and what makes the John Belushis, Ernest Hemingways, Sylvia Plaths, or Janis Joplins end up destroying themselves so tragically? The crucial distinction isn't between those Type Cs who succeed in the world and those who fail. It's between those who are in equilibrium with their craziness and those who are overwhelmed and even defeated by it. I vote for equilibrium.

shakespeare, *king lear*: Ripeness is all.
atchity: Yeah, but awareness don't hurt!

At its best and brightest, the Type C personality experiences exhilaration, laughter, and applause; at its darkest, despair and self-destruction. Above all, Type Cs value awareness. What is the difference between a functional Type C and a narcissist? The Type C is productive, with something to offer the world. The narcissist isn't. And, yes, sometimes it's hard to tell the difference. I learned very early in my career change that the greatest success I could hope to achieve wasn't necessarily to succeed in the eyes of the world, but to gain an understanding of the battle going on within me and master its forces, rather than allowing them to master me.

Along the journey of designing a life that successfully reflects your creative aspirations and dreams, part of the challenge is dealing with solitude and regularly being misunderstood. People who love to work all the time because they love their work are in the minority, and they're subject to the usual discrimination endured by minorities—fear, backbiting, hatred, envy, guilt trips—from authority figures, from peers, and from their own inner insecurities. I call these forces "the Accountants," from the "Continent of Reason" who command most of the space inside your mind (as described in my earlier book on creativity, *A Writer's Time: A Guide to the Creative Process, from Vision through Revision*). They're everywhere, always ready to judge where you are right now—when what's most important to you is where you're going. The authority figures in your life—your parents and teachers and bosses—aren't judging your progress or your potential; they're judging your present reality and past success. The worst of the Accountants will tell you, "People never change," unable to relate to your driving desire to do precisely that. Comparing your ancient Ford to their new BMWs, your friends and co-workers at your day job are judging that you've failed. When you explain that your dream is more important than your car, they can't bring themselves to believe you, as much as they'd like to, because of what it would say about them.

The worst Accountants are those within: the inner voices that tell you you're not measuring up (the sounds of your inner insecurity), judging you against a standard you internalized at a time when you were probably much too young to realize what you were doing. Faced with insecurity based on doing what no one else around you is doing, compounded by calumniation from relatives, friends, and neighbors; with rejection from the world you're working toward; your spirits may flag from time to time. How often? I once advised a client to forget about tomorrow; just worry about today.

"I'm worried about making it through the next hour," she said. "Okay," I replied. "Let's talk right now." We got her through it. I shared with her a poem I'd written years earlier:

Cracking Up Time

Last week
it was down to weeks.
By yesterday
it was days—hours,
by last night.
Now I make it
through each minute,
fearing
what measures
next.

It helped her to hear that her sense that the end of the world was upon her wasn't unique. Yes, the feeling that the end of the world is at hand comes often to the Type C personality embarked on what could, for all he knows, be a voyage into the abyss.

practice interminable patience
Technique and awareness allow you to proceed despite that feeling. And my first advice is to be patient. It takes five years, as an entrepreneur friend in New York points out, just to get used to the idea that there's no one out there who can help you as much as you can help yourself. As the Book of Job illustrates, almost nothing can conquer patience. Except persistence. Persistence is patience with a plan. In the words of Calvin Coolidge, "Press on."

form a long-range operating plan
Once you've formed your operating plan, patience and persistence become one and the same virtue. If you glean from the

experience of other dreamers insights that allow you to shape, strengthen, or maintain your master plan, you'll be well on your way to becoming an overnight sensation in ten years or less.

"Though this be madness," says Shakespeare's Polonius, "yet there is a method to it." I've always believed that planning to make it in the long run by firmly laying the proper tracks to your dream goal may make it happen sooner. In any case, whether sooner or later, laying down the correct tracks will make the goal happen regardless of luck. You can't build a game plan on luck. Meanwhile, while you're working away, with or without it, you're moving along tracks that you know are heading in the direction of your dreams. Take inspiration from Mahatma Gandhi's words:

> I know the path: it is straight and narrow. It is like the edge of a sword. I rejoice to walk on it. I weep when I slip. God's word is: He who strives never perishes. I have implicit faith in that promise. Though, therefore, from my weakness I fail a thousand times, I will not lose faith.

If you redefine success as continuous striving toward a worthwhile goal, even if you die before you get there, you'll be dying a happy death. And if you don't die, if you get to face another round of dragons tomorrow, you'll understand that merely surviving is part of your success. "I'll settle for surviving," you'll say to yourself because survival is the first important step toward achieving your goals.

embrace action as a long-term goal

Focus your energies by making the successful achievement of your creative lifestyle one of your long-term goals. Then, remind yourself that nothing can happen to the master plan, no matter what obstacles may be looming today. Move slowly, confidently, professionally toward your objectives. Before deciding that you're truly upset by a setback, ask yourself, Does this matter to the master plan? Does this truly affect my dream? If your goal is to succeed in ten years, or even in five, how can anything that happens today truly get you off track? Just make taking action a way of life, knowing that your energies are as boundless as your dreams.

learn to compromise today

If today forces you to compromise, compromise. But don't compromise with your dream; compromise *within* your dream. Adjust your objectives, not your goals. If the sidetrack you've been lured onto by the necessities of the moment, or forced onto by life's demands, strays from your dream, do your best to overcome its temptation and return to the path you've forged for yourself. No matter what the price. If the sidetrack seems to be running parallel, generally heading in the direction you want to go, then take it—as long as you're not fooling yourself about where it leads.

resist immediate gratification

Try as best you can to short-circuit the need for short-range, immediate gratification. Or, if you must have it, find it outside your dream. Sometimes people remain bound in the shallows and miseries of their lives because they're constantly choosing immediate gratification over delayed gratification. The ability to choose to delay gratification is the Type C's most powerful skill.

maintain your perspective

Sometimes, buried in the avalanche of the dream-monsters your creativity has unleashed, you'll think you're making little progress. Find ways to stand back far enough to accurately measure your progress. Creative systems of measurement are all around us. At one point, I told myself I'd make a film deal by the time my Pontiac's odometer reached 33,000 miles. At 32,000 miles, the odometer cable broke, no doubt touched by Mercury's magic wand. I decided not to repair it until the deal was made.

know thyself

them: Are you out of your mind?

us: Just the opposite. I'm only in my own mind. Whose mind are you in?

The legendary inscription, "Know thyself," above the portals of the oracle at Delphi must have been written for Type C personalities. Your strongest enemy is not the "No" you keep hearing over and over, but ignorance of the underpinnings of your own behavior, your own motivations, your own strengths and weaknesses. No self-help prescriptions can replace introspection. Introspection is the key to success in the daily task of making up your own mind. Albert Einstein defined insanity as repeatedly expecting different results from the same actions. Your artistic madness must not take this course if fulfillment is to be achieved. I consider my career change a true postgraduate education because, on a daily basis, it's forced me to confront myself in different ways. For the Type C, a happy life is inspired by the love of his dream and governed by his knowledge of self. The balanced Type C not only has a vision, but also the determination required to pursue that vision. We're lucky. Most people live in someone else's dream. We get to live in our own.

Self-investment means allowing your uniqueness to define your life, firmly refusing to let anything else define it. Marsha Sinetar, in her provocative *Ordinary People as Monks and Mystics*, compares the creative personality's lifestyle to that of a monk. Every part of your life—from the moment you rise in the morning, through the countless times during the day when you seriously consider checking in for a lobotomy, until at last you find a way to quiet your demons enough to get a good night's sleep—is part of your design. I once lectured at the International Conference for Science Fiction in Trieste on what I called *auto-possessione*, "self-possession," as a theme in science fiction. That's what you're aiming for, consciously: to take possession of yourself, exorcizing all other spirits but your own from your being.

Along the way, it might help to know that the Type C personality has recognizable characteristics. If you ask, "How do I know for sure that I'm not crazy?" rest assured that your question is a normal Type C question. If you weren't asking it, you'd be in trouble. If you're filled with free-floating anxiety as you begin a new project, you're experiencing the normal sensations Type Cs feel at beginnings. I always tell my clients, "If you *weren't* anxious, I'd be worried about you," then cite the old Cajun saying, "If you ain't scared, you ain't doin' nothin' important."

3

accountant, visionary, and the mind's eye

walt whitman: Do I contradict myself? Very well then I contradict myself. (I am large. I contain multitudes.) **atchity:** But let's narrow the multitudes down to three.

How many times have you heard, from well-meaning not-so-well-meaning friends, "You're living in a dream world!"? That confrontation is particularly frightening because you've told yourself the same thing all too often. The practical, reasonable part of the Type C mind, the Accountant (my Dad), is always frightened when the Visionary, with its bright-eyed ambition (my Mom), seems to take charge of the day-to-day routine of living. These two voices are the left- and right-brain serpents that are constantly at war. Mercury's caduceus takes charge of your dream world by allowing you to discern which serpent voice is which. Only then can you learn how to conduct with the master's baton their never-ending dialogue.

The Accountant in all of us is the product of our puritanical culture. Accountants urge us to keep busy: Idle minds are the devil's workshop. Accountants are in charge of synchronizing clocks around the world. And the Accountant doesn't trust the Visionary because the Visionary has no idea what time it is on the Accountant's clock. The Accountant is the voice that, when it comes to words, keeps the alphabet in alphabetical order. When it comes to relationships, deals, sentences, paragraphs, proposals, activities—any structured matters whatsoever—the Accountant insists on "a place for everything, and everything in its place." The great niche maker and pigeonhole maker, he demands beginnings, middles, and ends. In that order. The Accountant insists on yes or no, black or white, either/or, 1 or 0; without him, we would have no computers. As far as your Accountant is concerned, a stoplight offers only two choices: green for go, or red and yellow for stop. If you've slammed into someone who stopped for a yellow light recently, you've slammed into your Accountant. The Accountant's primary goal and function in your life is survival first, longevity second, health third. You must choose chocolate *or* butterscotch syrup. At the end of each race, there's only one winner.

When it comes to time, the Accountant's allegiance is to every logical ordering device from Greenwich Mean Time to your digitized, waterproof, chronomatic, moon-cycle-sensitive, solar-powered wristwatch—and he demands that they be kept in sync regularly. The Dustin Hoffman character in the film *Rainman* is an example of a person whose brain has been taken over by its Accountant. When things go like clockwork, it's usually thanks to the Accountant's knowledge of the inner workings of clocks. He wants us to believe that he's eternal, ubiquitous, and omniscient. In the days before digital bedside alarm clocks, you could set your clock for 7:00 A.M. and inexplicably awaken just as the big hand moved to 12—before the alarm went off. Now, with digital time, you awaken at 6:59, just before the quartz display announces 7:00. Why? Because the Accountant never sleeps. He designed and controls your personal computer, always knowing what time it is whether you're on or off.

This dialogue from one of Johnny Hart's *B.C.* cartoons makes fun of the Accountant:

Caveman #1: You got the time?
Caveman #2: About noon.

Caveman #1: I'd prefer something more exact.
Caveman #2: About noon, stupid.

The Accountant doesn't even get the joke. He hates it when everyone else laughs. The Accountant is relentless, untiring, all-disciplined, retentive. But is he a genius? No. Is he inescapable? No. Is he truly eternal and ubiquitous? No. The Accountant controls only objective or logical time.

The Visionary is that force in the Type C's mind that controls the craziest voices, the voices of your dream islands. It's the voice of Hamlet's "undiscovered country," where brainstorms are the order of the day and light bulbs the order of the night. When it comes to the alphabet, the Visionary reaches into a hat and draws a letter: "Today is brought to you by the Letter M." The poet Howard Nemerov asked, "Who put the alphabet in alphabetical order?" to remind us of the Accountant's arbitrariness. Alphabetical order isn't essential; it's merely convenient to the orderly functioning of society.

When it comes to the pea trick at a carnival, the Visionary cheats: None of the shells have peas under them—or they all do. When asked if he believed that every film should have a beginning, a middle, and an end, Italian director Bernardo Bertolucci paused momentarily before answering, "Yes, but not necessarily in that order." To the Visionary, a yellow stoplight means challenge, living on the edge—Go faster! As for yes or no, the Visionary has no problem saying "yes *and* no," insisting on the simultaneous validity of opposing forces. When the Little Prince was asked if he wanted to take a boat or a train, he replied, "Yes, I would like to take a boat and a train." Why must I choose between chocolate or butterscotch when I want both? Is the Visionary disciplined? Not at all. Words like "disciplined," usually betrayed by their Latin roots, are almost always Accountant-centric words. Visionary words include "yum," "ai-yi-yi," "wow," "kee-yi!," and "eureka." The Accountant may be pompous and ponderous and excessively authoritative, but the Visionary can be mean, surly, and downright disrespectful. Visionaries call Accountants "bean counters." Accountants call Visionaries "lunatics."

When it comes to the Accountant's reality, the Visionary response is reflected in Liza Minnelli's whimsical line: "Reality is something you rise above."

Type Cs are, by definition, in the minority. You've chosen to listen to the distant drum of your Visionary inner voice—dedicating your life to being "artistic," "bohemian," "inventive," "idealistic," "mad dog," "maverick," "manic depressive," "impresario," "different," "weird"—all words the Accountant uses to describe you when you refuse to fit in. You are, it concludes, a square peg in a round hole. Your Accountant's idea of metaphor is cliché. "Listen to reason," the Accountants said to Joan of Arc. She refused. She was happier listening to her Visionary voices. And she was burned at the stake for being possessed. Looking at it from her perspective, Joan was *self*-possessed, with the courage of her visionary convictions and just enough entrepreneurial awareness to save France and make an eternal name for herself in history. Centuries later, she inspired a television series, "Joan of Arcadia." When the Accountants said, "You're only a girl," Joan replied, "Lead me to your army."

The Type C's Accountant would be much happier if you'd spend your every waking hour (loves those clichés!) working in a lucrative engineering position or a vested government management job, where he could count on a weekly or biweekly paycheck. The Accountant likes to know where the next meal is coming from. The moment he figures that out, he wants to know where the next one will come from, and so on. The Accountant is never satisfied, even secure in the vision of thousands of meals night after night on the same patio at the same grill until you're ready for retirement. "Then what will we eat?" he wants to know.

"Give us a break," you begin saying to yourself after you've lived long enough to know that meals aren't everything and a preplanned, thirty-year diet doesn't satisfy the soul. Your Visionary wants to be heard. The Accountant has been silencing him for all these years, finding justification for doing so by reasoning that the Visionary speaks with too many tongues, no fan of Walt Whitman's *Leaves of Grass*, "I am large. I contain multitudes." The Type C personality has as many ideas as the little old lady who lived in the shoe had children. If these visions are allowed free play, reasons the Accountant, they'll flood us with their diversity and disorganization and we'll end up starving. Yet the ideas, despite all the Accountant's efforts to contain them behind the dike, keep leaking out. What to do? Without the Visionary, your life would have no meaning.

competition, cooperation, and creativity in the triadic mind

Your dream world's stability depends on discovering that the Accountant and the Visionary aren't the only forces at play inside your Type C mind. If the mind were truly dualistic, we'd be in constant conflict, with no hope of turning competition into creative progress. But cooperation between the two warring serpents is possible because the mind is actually *triadic*. Like the dialectical process of thesis, antithesis, and synthesis, the internal process by which the mind thinks and acts in the world becomes most productive by the yoking together of opposites. The part of your mind that conducts the self-examination, that "knows itself," and maintains awareness on an ongoing basis by watching and observing, is what I call your "Mind's Eye" (I called this part of the writer's mind the "Managing Editor" in my earlier book *A Writer's Time*). Your Mind's Eye is illustrated on the back of the U.S. dollar bill—the mystical third eye that unites the two sides of the triangle.

Your Mind's Eye is well aware of the Accountant's anxieties, and respects them because it recognizes the Accountant's essential role in our physical and fiscal survival. On the other hand, it also respects the Visionary's struggle to make dreams come true. Your Mind's Eye's awareness is Mercury's caduceus, setting the serpentine yin and yang spinning black and white into the stable dynamism of gray. The Mind's Eye is our onboard salesperson, trickster, acrobat, mentor, ringmaster, lion tamer, alchemist, magician, thief, and negotiator, operating between the forces of nature represented by the two serpents. The Mind's Eye agrees that the Accountant stands to reason and that the Visionary inspires hope. The Mind's Eye understands that forward motion, or progress, has the best chance of occurring when two opposing forces are yoked together so their energies can work in tandem. Having done the research the Accountant is afraid to do, the Mind's Eye also knows that dreams can have tangible value in the real world, and that their value will never be realized unless a deal can be struck with the Accountant to let the Visionary out of the cave of imagination long enough to voice its ideas.

If the Accountant has been in charge of your mind up to now, you're mired in a rut, stuck on the treadmill, dying to break free. You're bored. If the Visionary has been in charge, you keep having great ideas that seem to go nowhere and are truly beginning to doubt your sanity. You're scared to death. Your Mind's Eye, the most lucid and helpful of the three parts of your mind, when you allow it to take over, also recognizes that you ("you" defined in logical terms as the integration of the three parts of your mind) can't be happy and productive until a world is constructed around you that allows the free pursuit of your visionary dream in an accountable way.

The Mind's Eye is the master of productive argument: Where the name-calling stops because the arguing parties, in their new creative trialogue, have come to agree that the purpose of their contretemps is to clear the air and reach an agreement on how best to move forward using the strengths of both sides of the mind. Based on this underlying contract, the contrary parties are now free to express themselves honestly and directly while your Mind's Eye listens, chooses the best or the complementary approach, and thanks them for their honesty and cooperation with your desire for progress.

Once it has been awakened and empowered, the Mind's Eye has two primary functions in your mind: It observes and it negotiates. Being aware that the Accountant is useful and the Visionary is perceptive, that the Accountant is objective and the Visionary subjective, that the Accountant is great at organizing while the Visionary is great at conceiving something worth organizing—these are the Mind's Eye's primary functions. Mastery begins with understanding, and understanding emerges from detached observation. The Mind's Eye is as fast as quicksilver (another word for mercury). You—the real you, the best you, the you you want to be, your authentic self—should be identified first and foremost with your Mind's Eye, observing what you're doing, what you're feeling, what you're thinking, what you're dreaming. Your Mind's Eye's power comes from understanding, and its power manifests itself in an ability to turn understanding and awareness into arbitration, dialogue, mediation. Others have called the Mind's Eye the "watcher within," or "the monitor," but, soulful as they may be, such terms are too passive.

"The Accountant has a valid concern," your Mind's Eye tells the Visionary. "If you spend all day every day sharpening your pencils, we'll all starve." Your Mind's Eye works out an agreement whereby the Accountant allows the Visionary to sharpen pencils for two hours a day, and the Visionary agrees to take weekends off and devote an extra hour a day to the day job until the project is finished. Your Mind's Eye enforces this contract, insisting that the Visionary use the last five minutes of your writing time to psych itself up for tomorrow's two hours by deciding what needs to be done next and carefully covering the computer keyboard. The Accountant agrees to turn its constant worrying off for the Visionary's designated two hours, reasserting itself only at one hour and fifty-five minutes. If it feels it can trust your Mind's Eye's contract, the Accountant even enjoys going off the meter for a spell. It can, at last, take a responsible rest. And during that rest, it may even learn to appreciate the value of what the Visionary is up to. But the Accountant will not cooperate with the Visionary without a firm contract negotiated by your Mind's Eye.

The Mind's Eye is aptly described in a letter written by choreographer Martha Graham to her student Agnes de Mille, who had asked to resign from her dance troupe because she felt inadequate:

> There is a vitality, a life force, an energy, a quickening that is translated through you into action. And because there is only one of you in all time, this expression is unique and if you block it, it will never exist through any other medium, and be lost. The world will not have it. It is not your business to determine how good it is, nor how valuable, nor how it compares with other expressions. It is your business to keep the channel open. You do not even have to believe in yourself or your work. You have to keep open and aware directly to the urges that actuate you. Keep the channel open.

Your Mind's Eye recognizes that the beauty or brilliance of the Visionary's idea can benefit from the form or structure provided by the Accountant—and keeps the channel open. Mercury is playing his role as psychopompos, escorter of souls, to take us where we dream of going because he sees all the Accountant's tricks, all the Visionary's tantrums and spells, and he feels confident that something can be found at the bargaining table to please everyone: a win–win scenario.

Your Mind's Eye is the lead horse in the troika, the one that says yes to chocolate, yes to butterscotch, but "Let's be mindful of the calories and have a half-portion of each." If you're not yet hearing that third, all-important voice in your mind, start listening for it now, and it will expedite your career change. The world created by your Mind's Eye is neither a crazy vision nor a realistic Accountant's world. It's your functional dream world.

A therapist I consulted during a crisis in my career change told me, "You have the most amazing capacity for sustaining self-delusion I've ever run across." On the way home that night, I realized that he hadn't meant it as a compliment. His comment marked him as an incorrigible Accountant. I switched therapists immediately because, for my Type C mentality, denial of reality was the necessary foundation for going beyond my previous capacity to achieve. Defining deniers as people who "minimize the seriousness of their condition through hope, optimism, and humor," the psychologist Thomas Hackett has measured their extraordinary ability to succeed and to survive in conditions that defeat those who more readily accept the constraints of world they inhabit.

Dream worlds are always anxiety-producing to the Accountants of the regular world, who are by far the majority, both in numbers and experience. The Type C's Mind's Eye must map the characteristics of his dream world if he wishes to achieve peace of mind, to find his niche. Unlike those with regular paychecks, whose characters are created externally, in response to the needs of society, the character of the Type C personality must be created internally, responding to his need to draw out his vision from within and sell it to society. He *creates* his niche. If creating a niche seems like an uphill battle as you design your dream, searching for its fulfillment, it's precisely because you're going against the stream. If it weren't uphill all the way, you'd probably be doing nothing creative. "Of course it's hard," Tom Hanks, playing the coach in *A League of Their Own*, declares, "If it weren't hard everybody would do it. The hard is what makes it great." My director friend Mort put it this way: "It's always an uphill battle—especially because we're not always sure the hill is there." The Accountants around you, and the Accountant within you, are constantly pressuring you to "join the group," "take a reality pill." The Visionary inside you refuses.

The Mind's Eye evolved in response to the human mind's two impulses—the thirst for vision and the need for practicality. Negotiating between these two contrary drives, the Mind's Eye pressures them both to work together toward productive, creative expression—without driving us crazy. The Mind's Eye provides method for your madness.

A client of mine started working with one of my companies, AEI, because she realized she'd been letting her life go by in a career that wasn't giving her the satisfaction she craved. The next time someone says, "You're living in a dream world! Your head is in the clouds," you should simply reply, "That's where I like it. And where, exactly, is your head?" Be proud of your dream world. It's truly your greatest creation.

coping with your ambition: energy versus experience

viktor frankl: What is to give light must endure burning.
atchity: And burn without burning up.

If you have literary ambition focused in a dream, you have the ability to cope with the obstacles to achieving that ambition and making that dream come true. It's a question of whether you choose to mine that ability or not. Those contemplating career transitions often hesitate because, as their Accountants know only too well, they're not getting any younger.

Unarguably, that's true for the Accountant, whether the Visionary agrees or not. But the Mind's Eye points out to the Accountant that for every diminution of energy you've experienced, you've increased your overall experience. Energy and experience are like the pistons in a two-piston engine. As the energy piston goes down, the experience piston goes up, producing a balance. That kind of balance allows the older, amateur tennis player to keep up with, and even beat, the younger. The self-confidence you gained from your first career is equal to the brashness you brought to that first career. The argument of age is unacceptable. You're capable of changing as long as you believe you can. Henry Miller was in his forties

when he published his first novel. Colonel Sanders began
franchising his chicken business at the age of sixty-five.

walking the tightrope

I once returned to Los Angeles from a lecture tour in northern
California to find a package from my mom awaiting me.
I opened it to find a very strange gift—strange because my
family normally gives only practical gifts. It was a clock unlike
any clock I'd seen before. Inside a transparent plastic box, an
acrobat was perched on a ball, his feet moving as fast as they
could, his hands holding a balance pole that marked the time.
I was amazed, and touched. My mother understood the
tightrope I was walking as I fashioned my dream world by fits
and starts.

In the years that followed, my doodles further explored the
tightrope—that straight line between two powerful opposing
forces. On one side of the rope (the future), I drew dreams-come-
true, such as:

- The production of my first script
- A client's manuscript receives a six-figure advance (first
  happened in 1996)
- The publication of my next book (happening regularly)
- A major star is attached to an AEI project (happened in
  1998)
- The long-range funding of my television company
  (an offer is now on the table)
- A client's book wins the National Book Award
- A client's script receives the Emmy
- A condo in Manhattan (happened in 1999)
- My own script receives an Oscar
- The first check for $1 million (happened in 1998)
- The first feature film shot at New York's Plaza hotel
  (happened in 2001)
- The farm in Louisiana

But these successful dreams, recorded in green, were surrounded by the red dragons of failure—which, until my Mind's Eye took charge, were high-anxiety, red-ink nightmares:

- Debts from my first excursions into business that threatened to swallow up all my current income
- An IRS auditor demanding a written explanation of every single phone call; etc.

Both the dreams and the serpentine dragons had allies, angels, and demons from the past. They wedged themselves beneath my feet on the tightrope in an area I couldn't see because you can't look directly beneath you, if you hope to avoid falling. The dragons were:

- The many projects that came within an inch of being realized, only to slip away into the ether
- Projects that died on the vine from lack of distribution, lack of financing, or lack of interest on the part of the audience for whom they were intended
- Partnerships that began with great expectations and ended in disappointment
- Relationships that had grown strained beyond the breaking point by the discrepancy between my vision of the future and the other party's inability to continue believing that our ship would come in

Those were the red dragons that lurked around every corner, salivating over the green dreams they desperately craved for breakfast, lunch, and dinner. The allies (past successes), though, were equally strong:

- Books published and well-received
- Films produced and distributed
- New screenplays developed and written
- Production contracts signed
- Relationships maintained and strengthened
- A business line of credit opened at the bank
- Debt retirements or settlements
- The avoidance of bankruptcy
- My two children completing college
- My granddaughter entering French school

I could point to these as evidence of hope and progress. Despite out-of-balance expenses, my gross income was greater most years in my new career than in my old, my source of ideas continued not only to increase but also to improve, and my contacts with distributors, financiers, and artists slowly but surely grew stronger each day. Broken relationships had been repaired. Past completion gave reasonable promise for future expectation.

Behind me on the tightrope were the people I'd identified as my positive support group—my family, my business colleagues, and myself. In front of me, in the direction I was, by necessity, always facing, were the next pay periods—the first of next month, the fifteenth, the first, the fifteenth. Echoing in the back of my mind were always these questions: Am I gambling intelligently with my talents or am I just plain crazy? Is this a calculated or a foolish risk? To counter these distracting and terrifying echoes, I repeated to myself, and to my support group for their corroboration, a forward-looking, positive mantra: "I have no doubt of my long-term success if I can continue maneuvering pay period by pay period through the short term." Since scaling the cliff wall looming above you is no more hazardous than negotiating the wall below or the ledge upon which you're standing, your best bet is to continue going for it!

4

what's the plan?

epictetus: First say to yourself what you would do, then do what you have to do.
atchity: Plans make dreams come true.

The most exhausting, challenging, and exhilarating part of my Type C entrepreneurial life is the constant need to reevaluate the operating plan. Even though control may be an illusion and fate—as much as our own actions—may determine the course of our lives, maintaining equilibrium and perspective in a sea of troubles demands a reference point. The reference point is the overall strategic operating plan you've decided, in your Mind's Eye, to pursue. My Mind's Eye has to rally me back to the dream quest by waving the operating plan in my face from time to time.

I've learned that if I don't do this constant reevaluation, if I allow myself to drift too long, my anxiety starts announcing itself in various parts of my body. Movable pains signal that I've been ignoring system distress. Having an active Mind's Eye on board has provided insight over the interaction between mind and body I would otherwise not have understood. Here's the pattern—the behavior pattern and interaction with the world that occurs when

I stray from my operating plan—I've noticed about myself. The warnings from my unconscious come in stages.

STAGE #1. Body pains, usually focused in my lower back. If I ignore them, the pressure to take notice of what's happening to me accelerates into Stage #2.

STAGE #2. Traffic "near misses" (although, as George Carlin points out, shouldn't they really be called "near collisions"?). I bump into the car in front of me at a stoplight, ever so gently but enough to snap me to attention. I scrape my hubcap against a curb. I hit the bulwark in the garage just hard enough to ding my front bumper. My unconscious is screaming for attention, and willing to pay for bodywork to get it. If I ignore these signs, the next stage occurs.

STAGE #3. I lose my wallet. If the detour from my path is serious, this can be a real loss—forcing me to get a new driver's license (I now keep two spares in my desk drawer), cancel credit cards, and so on. If it's less serious, the wallet will turn up as soon as I've stopped to regroup. But while I'm looking for it, without having come to the realization that these events are signs, my unconscious moves to the final level, Stage #4.

STAGE #4. I lose my glasses. Sometimes three pairs within the same twenty-four-hour period. Once, I was in New York on a new business detour for a few days before taking a much-needed vacation to Antigua with my daughter Rosemary, at the time a sophomore at Columbia College. She stayed at the Yale Club with me the two nights before we were to leave New York. I managed to lose my glasses at a Greenwich Village production of *Steel Magnolias*. Having been through this before, Rosemary patiently accompanied me to the bar we'd stopped at en route to the theater. No luck. Then to the theater itself. No luck.

After I lamented that I'd just bought these new "far-see" glasses, I finally gave up and returned to the Yale Club, determined to buy another pair first thing in the morning so I wouldn't be visionless at the beach. I asked my dreams to tell me where the glasses had been lost. When I got out of bed the next morning, I almost stepped on them. They were lying on the floor, at the head of the bed. The dream had gotten on its hands and knees and found them.

In Antigua, I lost them again on the beach. This time I didn't find them. Rosemary wanted to know why I was so intent on losing them.

"Because my unconscious is trying to tell me something," I explained.

"What?"

"That I can't see where I'm going."

And my unconscious was right. I resigned from the "detour" company I was working for the next month and went back to being on the direct track to my dream. Now every time I lose my glasses, I reevaluate the operating plan first, and look for them second.

An operating plan, constructed through your Mind's Eye's negotiation with the Accountant and the Visionary, is the overall relationship between goals and objectives with a built-in "revision factor" along the way:

- You will begin to taste that dreamed-of future happiness when you construct your plan to suit where you are at the moment.
- You'll have a better attitude toward your day job by clearly recognizing that it's primarily a means to an end.
- You'll be more compassionate about your family's pressing needs because you'll know you've found a long-range solution to your own needs.

- You'll be better able to deal with today's financial anxieties by recognizing that the calculated risk today will yield a profitable tomorrow.

Immense relief sets in when you extend your operating plan, without limitation, into the future. As Cynthia Whitcomb puts it, "Don't put deadlines on your career." Saying to yourself, "My dream is to create a nationwide franchise within three years," is an invitation to self-sabotage. What you should say instead is, "I'm going to make the best cookies I possibly can. That's the plan." You then proceed to set objectives along the way and to post target deadlines for accomplishing them—while, at the same time, posting reminders to yourself to revise those deadlines on a regular basis. That's exactly what Debbi Fields (of Mrs. Fields cookies) did. "In order to hit the duck," says Lee Iacocca, "you have to move your gun." If you set an unrealistic deadline for the accomplishment of your goal, your Accountant won't be convinced, no matter how confident your Visionary, nor how energetic your Mind's Eye.

How do we know what's realistic or unrealistic in a situation we haven't mastered before? That's precisely the point: We don't, so we can't set hard-and-fast deadlines. Even the Accountant knows you can't become a sensation overnight, at least not without extraordinary luck. You accomplish one objective after another until a goal is achieved: You learn what you need to learn, apply it in a low-risk situation as a test; then apply it for real, and so on.

If you've placed no upper limit on the achievement of the goal you've dreamed for yourself, your commitment is total. It's easier, you'll discover, to make a total commitment to a dream that has no deadline. But the dream will never be realized unless you take the next step in planning: setting objectives that do have deadlines, ones that are both challenging and realistic.

dreams? plans? goals? objectives? what's the difference?

Dreams are the foundation of your inspiration and energy, the baseline ambition of your Visionary, which has inspired you to take the risks you're taking. In other words, they are motivational expressions of the guiding vision. You can see yourself as the most talked about chef in New York, can feel it in your bones, can taste the success—all of this before a meal of your own design has ever found its way to a restaurant table.

Dreams come first. With the help of an operating plan, those dreams can become realities.

Making them come true requires two things: commitment and the plan itself. Commitment marries your dream to your mission in life; you are going to make your dream your mission. The German poet-philosopher Johann Wolfgang Goethe made the most powerful statement about commitment I've ever run across:

> Until one is committed, there is hesitancy, the chance to draw back, always ineffectiveness. Concerning all acts of initiative [and creation] there is one elementary truth, the ignorance of which kills countless ideas and splendid plans: that moment one definitely commits oneself, then Providence moves, too. All sorts of things occur to help one that would never have otherwise occurred. A whole stream of events issues from the decision, raising in one's favor all manner of unforeseen incidents, meetings, and material assistance which no man would have dreamed could have come his way.
>
> Whatever you can do or dream you can, begin it. Boldness has genius, power, and magic in it. Begin it now.

Decisiveness, according to Lee Iacocca, is the primary quality of a good manager. But without planning, decisiveness is hamstrung. Now that we've begun, we need a campaign plan, consisting of general goals (strategy) and specific objectives (tactics). Like dreams, plans should contain deadlines but should not be governed by them. Let's say your dream is to be a produced screenwriter. As long as you're moving generally in that direction, nothing can take the dream away. But the plan recognizes that dreams come true step by step, and it focuses on the first step: learning about, conceiving, writing, rewriting, and marketing the first screenplay.

A plan consists of *goals* reached by *objectives* to be accomplished within a specific time frame laid out on an *agenda*. Objectives and goals have deadlines. Dreams don't.

operating plan

Dream: To be a produced screenwriter.
Current Situation: Working as a teller in the bank.
Goal: To finish my first screenplay within 24 months.

AGENDA

DEADLINES	OBJECTIVES	NOTES
During Month 1	Research continuing education catalogs	Do during lunch breaks; one or two hours weekly
By start of Month 2	Enroll in evening screenwriting class	Choose instructor who has Hollywood experience
	Read produced screenplays	Spend three hours weekly; one hour during lunch break on M, W, F
	Subscribe to *Writers' Guild of America Journal*	

continued...

AGENDA (continued)

DEADLINES	OBJECTIVES	NOTES
Start of Month 3	Revise this agenda	Don't forget to schedule when!
	Have private meeting with instructor (preferably lunch)	Ask him for advice on building your career
	Watch five movies	Use stopwatch to note when events occur in the ninety- to ninety-five-minute films
Start of Month 4	Revise this agenda	
	Check on liquidity of CDs	

Your plan will reflect the individuality of your dreams and goals, but don't forget to remind yourself that a to-do list has limited usefulness if you don't know *when* you're going to do it. An agenda consists of things to be done in a particular time frame.

Note that your second month limits the hours devoted to your dream to eight or nine, including the evening class. Your Accountant is happier when you ease gradually into the dream quest. You revise the agenda monthly in order to maintain your perspective; the agenda is working for you, you're not working for the agenda. Your revisions will be based on your successes and setbacks during the previous month. Did you fail to accomplish any of the objectives? Did you fail to spend the time you had planned? If so, set your objectives lower this month and your chances of success will be higher. The process is one of constant self-discovery and reevaluation. But between the reevaluations, do your best on a daily basis to accomplish the objectives you've set for yourself.

When you feel the need for inspiration, go to the library and research success stories. You'll more than likely discover that the men and women you'd choose as role models moved toward success through a series of what others would define as failures and constantly revised their perspective along the way. "A professional writer," Richard Bach says, "is an amateur who didn't quit."

But because you've placed no deadline on the dream itself, you'll realize—once you regroup after a setback—nothing that happens today can interfere with the operating plan. Your built-in revisions will provide for those unforeseen emergencies. Setbacks are considerations, not impediments. You'll be able to move slowly, firmly, and professionally toward that goal on the receding future horizon because nothing in the present can take it away from you. Before reacting strongly to each "No," you'll be able to tell yourself, "This doesn't matter in the long run, so to what benefit can I turn it?"

Does all this planning guarantee that you'll be in control? We all know the truth about this one: No one's ever in control. But life is bearable when we have a sense of being in control; referring to an operating plan allows us to set attainable goals, no matter how small, on a daily basis. Let's say we're working on a particular objective, because we have a goal, and see what results we can create in doing so. Then we'll correct our course of action depending on our observation of those results. As we move forward in this fashion, notice that what begins as hypothesis often ends in reality.

The important thing is to create a plan for your success that will allow you to keep the daily setbacks in perspective. What separates the successful people from those who haven't yet attained their goals is a fully detailed plan that allows them to visualize that success—and persistence. What will you do when you've received that first check for $1 million? If you don't know, or find yourself resisting that visualization, you may be up against a self-sabotaging fear of success (often indistinguishable from "fear of failure") that must be confronted and overcome. The operating plan details how you'll spend the money; how much you'll save for the freedom you've been seeking, and how much you'll use to retire debts and take care of other responsibilities. Some people reach the reward, only to squander it all by going into debt buying presents for themselves and friends, which explains the bumper sticker that reads, "Dear God, Please let me make one more sale and I promise I won't piss it away!" The writer of this plaintive cry learned the hard way that, when the money comes, the first priority must be to buy freedom for future creative endeavor. If that means continuing to struggle to pay the weekly bills, then so be it. You've become good at that struggle, so why stop just because you have the money now? It's a truism that affluent people are sometimes the last to fork over their money or pay their bills. Maybe that's why they're affluent.

The plan begins, of course, with where you are right now. It should cover all areas of your life and activities: your health, your family, your social life, your financial status, and your professional accomplishments. While the operating plan should extend at least seven years into the future, I've written plans that have covered me up to age ninety, just for the fun of it and to show myself how much time might be available. Taking the long view of time helps you acknowledge just how much can be done in whatever span of time you think you have left.

Here's an example from a seven-year plan for a single mother in Kansas City moving on a fast-track (because she's dreamed about doing this for years) from being a nurse to fulfilling her dream of writing for Hollywood. Here's her situation:

- She's thirty pounds overweight.
- Her cholesterol is too high.
- She has $20,000 in her savings account at the time she sits down to write the plan.

- Her daughter is now seven, in school full-time.
- Nurses are in demand, and she can more or less choose her hours.

Her list of objectives, of course, will be revised and/or expanded at revision points along the way. She writes the first draft of her operating plan on August 1; and she'll revise and fine-tune it once a month, on the first of each month. She'll keep her day job for the first six months; at that point, if everything's on track, she'll move to nursing part-time, scheduling her hours to accommodate her writing career.

operating plan for a career in hollywood

Dream: To sell my first spec script for $1 million or more, own a home in Westport Landing, and travel the world writing exciting stories in interesting places.

Current situation: Working as a nurse

Goal: To earn a comfortable living selling screenplays and story ideas.

More immediate goal: To sell my first screenplay.

1. Research Continuing Education courses on screen-writing *(COMPLETE by September 10)*
2. Build a research library of directories and catalogs *(ONGOING, but have the most important volumes on hand by October 15)*
3. Continue screenwriting efforts on weekends, reading as many produced screenplays as I can get my hands on, finding successful screenwriters I can talk to *(ONGOING)*
4. Enroll in two screenwriting courses *(COMPLETE by September 15)*
5. Complete both courses *(COMPLETE by January)*
6. Construct budget in terms of needs and resources *(ONGOING, but COMPLETE first draft by October 1)*

7. Complete redesigning my work space *(ONGOING, but COMPLETE by January 30)*
8. Plan first trip *(ONGOING, but book tickets by January 30)*
9. On trip, figure out my first story line *(COMPLETE by February 28)*
10. Plan the agenda for writing the first draft, which should take no longer than ten days once I've gotten the story straight in my mind *(COMPLETE first draft by April 1)*

She's decided that this is as far as she needs to plan her detailed agenda in advance, but her operating plan will also chart her present view of what might happen in the next six years, including planning to revise that first draft at least three times (with vacations in between).

Of course, she'll alter her plan as she gains information. Her plan makes her Accountant a little nervous because it foresees only six months in detail; but this woman has been listening to her nervous Accountant for years and has finally realized that the Accountant is always going to be nervous. She's also figured out that if she continues working at least part-time, her savings will carry her for at least another three years.

AGENDA (hpw—hours per week)

BY/HPW	PERSONAL OBJECTIVES	MONEY OBJECTIVES	WORK OBJECTIVES
9/10 (10 hpw)	Get weight to 120 and cholesterol to 220 by exercising three hours weekly on a low-fat diet	Add $4,000 to savings	• Choose courses on screenwriting/ marketing • Continue making notes on first screenplay

continued...

AGENDA (continued)

BY/HPW	PERSONAL OBJECTIVES	MONEY OBJECTIVES	WORK OBJECTIVES
9/15 (15 hpw)		Do two hours overtime to pay for housekeeper/ baby-sitter (seven extra hours)	• Enroll in courses at Longview Community College • Collect "library" • Work on budget
10/1	Maintain 120 weight		• **Revise this agenda** • Complete draft of budget • Research trip (choose part of country) • Buy best scriptwriting program
10/15	Get cholesterol to 215		• Assess library • Plan what books to get as well as screenplays of favorite movies
11/1	Get weight to 118	Savings at $25,000	• **Revise this agenda**
12/1	Maintain weight at 120 through holidays (exercise four hours weekly, hour one can be done by walking)		• **Revise this agenda** • Start designing workspace

continued...

AGENDA (continued)

BY/HPW	PERSONAL OBJECTIVES	MONEY OBJECTIVES	WORK OBJECTIVES
			• Take 12/5–1/1 as vacation from this operating plan
1/1 (20 hpw)	Maintain weight at 120	Savings at $23,000; Find a backup investor if career doesn't start paying for itself by 1/1 of next year	• **Revise this agenda** (inserting detailed budget) • Complete courses • Book tickets for trip
1/30			• Complete workspace and computer setup
2/1	Get weight to 115		• **Revise this agenda**
2/28 (40 hpw)			• Complete trip
3/1 (20 hpw)	Get cholesterol to 210		• **Revise this agenda** • Type favorite screenplay into new program as a test-run • Buy AEI tape "Writing Your Story in 3 Weeks"
3/15			• Listen to AEI tape twice

continued...

AGENDA (continued)

BY/HPW	PERSONAL OBJECTIVES	MONEY OBJECTIVES	WORK OBJECTIVES
4/1	One hour (or more) weekly swim		• **Revise this agenda** • Set one-week agenda for getting story plot straight
4/7			• Take one-week vacation from project to get psyched up • Buy 1,000 index cards, per tape's instructions
4/15 (25 hpw)			• Finalize story plot • Fill out the 1,000 cards
4/22	Arrange for babysitting for next week		• Take vacation to get psyched up for writing first draft • Book a hideaway for next week where I can work undistracted
5/1 (40 hpw)			• **Revise this agenda** • Get the first draft down!
5/8			• Take a vacation from project • Routine life back on track

continued...

AGENDA (continued)

BY/HPW	PERSONAL OBJECTIVES	MONEY OBJECTIVES	WORK OBJECTIVES
5/15 (20 hpw)			• Begin revising screenplay
6/1			• **Revise this agenda**
6/15			• Finish first revision by end of week • Begin notes and create agenda for second screenplay
7/1			• **Revise this agenda** • Start second revision of first screenplay
8/1			• **Revise this agenda** • Finish second revision of first screenplay
			• Get two reads from supportive acquaintances
8/15			• Tweak screenplay based on the reads
8/22			• Ask instructor to read screenplay.

She hasn't projected what her income might be at the end of the first year because she knows she can't possibly predict it accurately. With her nursing to fall back on, she figures she can get by. And her goal isn't to get rich screenwriting; it's to earn a comfortable living selling stories to Hollywood. She's learned enough about life to recognize that if she pours herself into her dream, she'll either get lucky or she won't. She has no control over luck, but she can control the time she devotes to the writing and the time she devotes to her day job.

The question her Mind's Eye brings into focus is this: "Can I somehow make it through the next seven years if I know that by then I'll be doing nothing but writing for Hollywood?" If the answer is no, she needs to adjust the agenda, shorten the space between objectives, find more time to work on her new career. If the answer is yes, all she needs is to begin immediately, and to polish the plan monthly as she acquires more information about her new career. The answer, by the way, is yes—if others have done it, she can do it too.

The goal she's set for herself provides focus for creating an agenda by which specific objectives can be reached that will inevitably take her to the goal. Because she schedules time for revising her goal—and the agenda required to reach it through objectives with deadlines—she'll stay in control of the process instead of letting the process take control of her. She's decided at the outset that she'll take one full day off every weekend to spend with her daughter. Her agenda also includes time for sloughing off and just relaxing, both over the December holidays and before she sits down to write her first draft. After all, she wants to treat herself like a human being, not an automaton unable to do anything except work. On the other hand, she may have scheduled fewer vacations than someone else in transition. As far as this woman is concerned, she's wasted too much time dreaming already. She feels the need to act on her dream.

Your objectives, revised as you learn more about your capabilities and as your luck changes, are the individual steps over which you have the greatest degree of control. After an internal trialogue among Accountant, Visionary, and Mind's Eye, you exercise control by fulfilling a pact with yourself to put in the amount of time you've decided makes sense at that stage in the operating plan. In order to keep the Accountant from feeling overly threatened, this woman has decided to spend no more than fifteen hours a week on her new career for the first few months, then ease into more hours per week as she comes closer to finishing her first script. If you take a gradual approach and stick to your time pact, you'll discover that the Accountant has become your strongest ally once he's satisfied that this might all make sense and actually lead to something. He'll be knocking on your writing office door, urging you to devote more time to this exciting new career.

What you've done is simply used all the parts of your mind to translate your belief in yourself into an operating plan that allows you to bring your dream into focus, while also giving the dream the room it needs to grow and evolve.

Let me emphasize the revision aspect of the operating plan with T. S. Eliot's observation: "The only method is to be very, very intelligent." Although operating plans are necessary as visualization aids, as philosophical underpinnings, and as placebos for the Accountant, the truth is that life itself has very little patience with rigid plans. By nature, the aspiring Type C will recognize and take advantage of unforeseen opportunities that have been generated by his decisive efforts to move in the direction of the dream. The career will evolve, and it would be a terrible mistake to stick to a preconceived plan when an exciting and immediate crossroads involves leaving the plan behind or altering the dream.

On her first research trip to Cajun country, our new screenwriter runs into an aspiring producer who's looking for a writer willing to write "on spec" (that is, on speculation). They work out an exchange whereby she writes a treatment of the story he wants to produce, and he agrees to raise money to pay her to write the script. She now has a second project, before she's even begun writing her first. At this point, the original operating plan is subordinated to the new opportunity generated by the nurse's dream. But the change fills her with exhilaration because it proves that fortune has smiled on her dream.

5

stealing time for your dream

jack smith: God created time so that everything wouldn't happen at once.
atchity: Then how come everything keeps happening at once?
accountant: You're living on borrowed time.
mind's eye: And since you don't have to pay time back, you can afford to enjoy it!

Follow your dream, and, by definition, you can't fail. Success lies in the following. If you have a dream, you have the responsibility to yourself and to the source of dreams to make it come true. That means finding time to do what you have to do—the very opposite of marking time. Our minds experience life on a timeline of their own invention, a continuum that stretches from our first moment of consciousness to our last. "The end of the world," said Bernard Malamud, "will occur when I die. After that, it's everyone for himself." The human mind is like a time bomb, ticking away and trying to find time—until it finally explodes.

And finding time in our accelerated world where we hear of flextime, time-elasticity, the sweet spot in time, virtual time, time shifting, and time slowing down is more confusing than ever before. A little over a century ago, if you missed a stage-coach you thought nothing of waiting a day or two for the next one to come along. Today you feel frustrated if you miss one section of a revolving door! So many of today's time-saving devices prove to be frauds—requiring more time to select, install, maintain, and update than it used to take without them. It's hard to believe that a few short years ago we had not yet become addicted to fax machines, microwaves, DVD players, headsets, cell phones—and even voicemail, email, and answering machines! All these inventions, as helpful as they can be to the Accountant's output level, suck up our time in ways that, unless they are examined and acknowledged, become quite destructive to the realization of the dream. More and more demands are being made on our time. Faith Popcorn (in her *Popcorn Report*) puts its this way:

> We're pleading to the big time clock in the sky: "Give me fewer choices, far fewer choices. Make my life easier. Help me make the most of my most valued commodity— the very minutes of my life."

It's time for the romance with Faster to come to an end, time to demand back the time that the gods of Fast have taken from us.

Things have gotten so bad that we can't really *manage* time any more. We're now forced to *steal* it, invoking the assistance of Mercurius Caduceator: messenger, salesman, trickster, and *thief* of the gods. Like any professional thief, Mercury insists on knowing as much as possible about the object of his theft and its natural habitat and characteristics before he springs into action. This chapter combines observations about the nature of time and work, with practical suggestions about employing Mercury's caduceus to steal the time you need.

bokonon: Busy, busy, busy.
ecclesiastes: Consider the ants. Yes, you are busy. What are you busy about?
atchity: Does this mean I have to know what I'm doing all the time?

Our puritanical upbringing has led the Accountant to want us to keep busy. "Idle hands are the devil's workshop." One day I was consulting with an attorney who, by everyone's standards but his own, is quite successful. We were talking about forming a new marketing company. "Why do you want to do this?" I asked him.

"Because I want to get rich." He added, "I have to stop selling my time."

I nodded. "That's interesting." I was thinking of the reversible equation I'd written about in *A Writer's Time*: "Time is money, money is time."

"What brought you to this conclusion?" I asked him.

He told me that a self-made, wealthy, genius friend of his kept coming to California for a visit. Each time, he'd say, "You're so smart, why aren't you rich?" The attorney had no answer for him, but the question continued to gnaw away at him.

Finally, on one visit, the friend had to sit in the attorney's office for an hour waiting for him to complete some phone calls. He observed what was happening in the office. On their way to lunch, his friend said, "You know that question I've been asking you all these years?"

"Yeah, of course I remember it—it drives me crazy. 'If I'm so smart, why aren't I rich?'"

"I know the answer now."

"Tell me."

"You're too busy to be rich."

Doing the wrong things, no matter how fast or how well you do them, or how many of them you do, will not advance your dream. One of my partners puts it this way: "Don't confuse efforts with results."

Those who break out of busy work and into the success they've dreamed of have learned to redefine time. If you recognize that time is merely a concept, a social or intellectual construct, you can make the clock of life *your* clock; then determine what you do with it. More than the quantity of activities or completed projects I've experienced in my career transit, what I value most is the quality of time I've managed to steal from all those committees and examination-grading sessions. When someone asked me a few years ago to make a list of things I do that I don't enjoy, I was happy to realize that it was difficult to think of anything other than my two or three hours per week of desk work that I don't thoroughly enjoy. Now I've found a way of enjoying deskwork, too! I've managed to steal, for the most part, the right kind of time for *my* dream.

what is time?

Unlike oxygen, an element which is objectively, scientifically definable, and more or less beyond our control, time is relative to perception and subject to choice. "Time," Herman Melville wrote, "began with man." The Type C learns to redefine time subjectively, in order to become successful by his own standards. Objective time, dictated by Greenwich Mean Time with an occasional correction for NASA, leads only to the conformity of repetition. Subjective time alone allows us to distinguish ourselves and to achieve our dreams of success.

LOGOS VERSUS MYTHOS

According to the classical Greeks, the two primary ways of perceiving the world were known to them as *logos* (the Accountant's logic) and *mythos* (the Visionary's simultaneity). The Visionary's belief in eternity is what makes the Type C's life change from barely bearable to ever enthusiastic. "To himself," Samuel Butler wrote, "everyone is immortal. He may know he is going to die, but he can never know that he is dead." The Visionary's eternity is the experience of *mythic time* that occurs when you lose yourself in the pursuit of your dream. It's Brer Rabbit's briar patch speech: "Throw me anywhere, but please don't throw me in the briar

patch!" The briar patch, of course, is Rabbit's favorite place—
his home.

Have you ever had the experience of bumping into an old
schoolmate and felt that "it was just yesterday" you were having
the exact same argument or laughing over something known
only to the two of you? A moment passes, as the Accountant
wrests control from the Visionary: "But, on the other hand, it
seems every bit like the twenty years it's actually been." *Has* it
been twenty years, or *was* it just yesterday? William Faulkner said:
"There is no such thing as *was;* if *was* existed, there would be no
grief or sorrow." To the Visionary, time exists always in the
present.

ACCOUNTANT'S TIME

To the Accountant, who's kept precise track of the years—and also
the month, weeks, days, hours, minutes, and seconds— it's been
exactly twenty years, and he can prove it by reciting all the things
that have happened to both of you in the interim. The Accountant
clocks time with digital precision, obsessive call-ins to the phone
company's correct time service. The Accountant's time is what
keeps society sane, if you call today's society sane. "Let's check our
watches."

But when the Accountant's insistence dominates, you cannot
make your dreams come true. The Accountant, nervous about
anything intangible or unseen, doesn't believe in dreams; or, at
best, assumes the worst about them: "They're only dreams."
Human beings can't fly.

VISIONARY TIME

To the Visionary, whose relationship with that same friend is/was
intense, it's just yesterday. The Visionary clocks time only by reference to intensity. Lovers live from embrace to embrace, the time
that's passed between them not counting. Have you ever felt as
if life were passing you by when you were stuck in an endless

lefthand-turning lane during rush hour? How long does a second last if you're perched at the parachute door of a plane at fifteen thousand feet about to make your first jump? How long is forty seconds during an earthquake measuring 6.6 on the Richter scale? Or at the edge of a cliff, where you are about to rappel for the first time? A friend of mine described an encounter with a prospective client this way: "I spent an eternity with her for an hour and a half yesterday."

The Visionary brings you mythic time when you engage in your career transit with all your heart, mind, and soul, when you are occupied in doing something that takes you out of time, or takes you out of yourself. You're *ecstatic*—which, from its Greek origins, literally means, "standing outside" yourself. "I don't know where the time went" is what you say when you've just spent fourteen hours creating the whole magical kingdom of *Tumbukti* and its graphics—and your spouse, sent by her worried Accountant to tell you you've missed an important dinner party, is banging on the door because you've taken the phone off the hook. Like Alice's White Rabbit, the Accountant would always have you believe that you're late for a very important date. And the Accountant doesn't like it one bit when your Mind's Eye stops to question how important that date may be, or whether you made the date in the first place or whether it was made for you. Type Cs insist on making their own dates because their Mind's Eyes have learned how to ensure that mythic time gets preference over logical time.

You've had this experience: You've told yourself you're just going to steal two hours to work on your dream. You go into the briar patch. One hour and fifty-five minutes have gone by, during which you've been lost—fully engrossed in your writing, without a thought for the outside world that operates on the Greenwich clock. The hours have passed like a minute (the Visionary's way of talking makes the Accountant crazy). Then, you look up at the clock to discover that only five minutes remain of your bargained-for two hours. How did you know to look up at the five-minute mark? Because your Accountant never sleeps, even when he's been taken off duty. If you decide to remain in the mythic time of your dream work beyond the five minutes remaining—that is, beyond the two hours you set aside—the Visionary has won this particular encounter. The Accountant has lost. If you decide to quit on time, you may think the Accountant has won, and the Visionary has lost.

What's wrong with this win-lose scenario is that it's exhausting, and impossible to maintain in the long run. Most people, faced with this constant, natural conflict between the two aspects of their minds, allow, as the only peaceful alternative, the Accountant to take over entirely. They choose the Accountant's conservative, safe way of behaving because the daily battle is too costly in terms of energy and emotion. If the Visionary wins the five-minute battle, for example, and you continue working on your new invention for another four hours instead of the two you'd set aside, guess how hard it's going to be for the Accountant to agree to the next two hours you want to steal. The Accountant will use every instrument in the arsenal of procrastination to postpone the trip to the workshop.

how to avoid losing time

francesco petrarch: It is appointed for us to lose the present in the expectation of the future.

atchity: The present: Use it, or lose it.

Petrarch, the first "Renaissance man," was aware that we spend a large majority of our time somewhere else other than in the present moment. Planning for the future, worrying about the past—so much so that by the time you reach middle age the two horses, Past and Future, are engaged in a life-and-death race along your internal time line. Competing for your vitality, stealing your present. The time you spend on past responsibilities, past regrets, past relationships, eats into the time available for growth and progress toward your future goals.

If we don't recognize what's going on here, as Accountant time and Visionary time battle in our perceptions, we can get very confused. When we get confused, the Accountant can take control of our lives. For most people, the Accountant is always in full control. Consequently, they are frustrated, bored, caught in a rut. With the help of Mercury's powerful caduceus—whose two snakes represent, as in my dream, the taming of past and future around the strength of present awareness—the entrepreneur's now-open Mind's Eye can transform the bloody battlefield into the altar of your hopes and dreams. Awakening his Mind's Eye, Jack London said:

> I shall not waste my days in trying to prolong them.
> I shall use my time.

This anti-Accountant declaration is made by your Mind's Eye—which knows that only by marrying the Accountant's logic to the Visionary's myth will the present be captured for effective dream work, in lieu of the Visionary wasting the present in daydreaming, or the Accountant in obsessing about the past and the future. When your Mind's Eye takes charge of these constant time wars, productivity combines with peace of mind. The photographer Ansel Adams said, "I'm amazed at how many people have emotional difficulties. I have none. If you keep busy, you have no time for them."

work management doesn't work

Time and work are essentially opposites. Here are the laws of time/work physics:

- **Time is finite**. We only live so long and, while we're alive, we have only twenty-four hours in every day.
- **Work is infinite**. Work, whether good or bad, always generates more work, expanding to fill the time available.

Given these physical laws, it should be obvious that work is unmanageable; that only time can be managed. Yet people regularly sabotage themselves by trying to manage work. "First I'll catch up with my day job, then I'll take time for my dream," or, "First, I'll get my family in good shape, then I'll find time for myself."

Don't get me wrong. Work is what we're trying to find time for. Writers write. Craftsmen make tables or boats or flower arrangements. Actors and models go for auditions and interviews. Salespeople make sales calls—the more calls they make, the more sales they make. Shakespeare's observation that "action is eloquence," is not only creatively productive, it's the best way to stay sane. Even one phone call a day in the service of your career transit means two hundred calls a year, if you take two days off each week. That's definitely progress. Success comes inevitably on the heels of constant work, as the ancient Greek poet Hesiod pointed out in his almanac: "If you put a little upon a little, soon it will become a lot."

My mentor Tom Bergin (Sterling Professor of Romance Languages and Master of Timothy Dwight College at Yale) was the author of fifty-nine books by the time he retired and eighty-three by the time he died. Yet he described himself as a "plodder." He just kept plodding away, in the vein of Hesiod. Tom and I exchanged dozens of letters from the time I left Yale to the time he died. He taught me the relentless equation between consistent, minor actions and ultimate productivity. One day, by way of complaining about having no time to do any serious work because of all the trivial errands and duties he had to attend to, he sent me a quotation from Ralph Waldo Emerson: "Things are in the saddle and ride mankind."

Against the accelerating incoming bombardment of the things of contemporary life, Type C work happens only when we *steal time* to make it happen. Yet schedules, to-do lists, self-revising agendas are constantly being tested and found insufficient. They work for a while, then become ineffective. Without recognizing this reality, through the Mind's Eye's awareness, each time this happens it may send us into a tailspin that moves us further from success. Life delights in creeping in to sabotage our dreams if only to make sure we're serious about them. One of my clients, after six months of working together to change her habits to become more productive, told me I was the "Ulysses S. Grant of time management." She told me that Grant sent Abraham Lincoln a telegram stating, "I plan to hammer it out on this line if it takes all summer." Others read this telegram before it was handed to the beleaguered president. The jealous snoops told Lincoln, "You know, we have reports that General Grant drinks a considerable amount of whiskey." "Is that right?" Lincoln replied. "Find out what brand he drinks and send a case of it to each of my generals." Lincoln recognized that whiskey was Grant's caduceus.

the human nature of time
archimedes: Give me a lever and I can move the world.
atchity: Time is the Type C's lever.

All you need to make your dreams come true is time. Using time as your most faithful collaborator begins with understanding its interactive characteristics and protean shapes. You'll begin noticing that time behaves differently under different circumstances. When you're concentrating, your awareness of time seems to disappear because you've taken yourself out of the Accountant's time and are dealing with the Visionary, whose experience is timeless. When you're away from your writing, you become very conscious of time because your Visionary is clamoring in his cage to be released from the constraints of logical time.

"you've got my full attention": compartments of time, time and energy, rotation, kinds of time, and linkage
Time-effectiveness is a direct function of attention span. When you're concentrating, giving the activity you're involved with your full attention, you produce excellent results. When your attention span wavers and fades, the results diminish. Until you recognize that attention span dictates effectiveness, you're likely to waste a great deal of time.

   The key to avoiding this situation is assessing how long your attention span is for each activity you engage in—and then doing your best to engage in that activity in appropriate compartments (allotments of time that you've found to be most productive). Since my particular career is multivalent, I pursue what I call a "rotation method" of moving among activities that support my producing, managing, writing, and speaking. I love all these activities, but not when I do them exclusively—each one having its own high ratio of crazy-making aspects that diminishes automatically when that activity is juxtaposed with the others.

Except during a crisis in one of the four areas, at which point all other activities stand aside until the crisis is resolved, I find it stimulating to spend an hour working on production-related matters, then spending the next hour on calls that manage various client projects in development. I've also learned that it's a waste of time to try to control things that only time can accomplish—such as making a phone call, then waiting next to the phone for a response to it; or staring at the toaster waiting for the toast to pop up. The only time you have anything approaching direct control of anything is when the ball is in your court. During that moment I focus on getting the ball out of my court into someone else's court so that I've done what I need to do to make the game continue.

Rotating from one activity to another ensures that the outreach begun in activity A will be "taking its time" while I'm engaged in activities B, C, and D. When the phone rings from the A call, I interrupt D to deal with it—and it's generally a pleasant interruption, knowing that one facet of my career is vying with another for my attention.

An hour is probably my average attention span compartment for work. But the length of the particular compartments (remember that "compartments" are allotments of time given to a particular work activity) changes from time to time as my attention span for that activity evolves. During the original drafting of this book, for example, I spent two hours a day writing, whereas before I began the draft my attention span allowed me to spend only an hour or less a day thinking about the book and gathering my notes for it.

There's no magical formula for determining attention span; it changes as you and your circumstances change. Yet once determined, attention span is the mastering rod between the serpents, the compartment of time where past and future meet in a present that feeds from the former and nourishes the latter.

Attention span is related to your energy level at different times of day, and with regard to different activities. Activities that drain you should not be scheduled one after the other, but should alternate with activities that generate energy for you.

Energy and attention span will also be different depending on whether you are at the beginning, in the middle, or at the end of a particular objective. Your attention span is most in danger of sabotaging you in the middle, where it's easy to confuse your fatigue from the hard work of plodding forward with some sort of psychological upset caused by the process you're engaged in. Usually shortening the allotments of time you're devoting to the present objective, or changing the activities around which you're scheduling this objective's compartments, can resolve that situation.

When a particular compartment is nearing its end, use the last few minutes of it (when the Accountant comes back to remind you that the time is almost up) to jot down what you're going to do the next time you revisit this compartment. This automatically puts your Visionary and Accountant into a percolation mode in which they bat things back and forth in the back of your mind while you're busy working in the next activity's compartment.

where does the time go?
the nonproductive type c: I don't know where the time goes.
once your mind's eye takes over: It doesn't go anywhere; time's in your face all the time! It's knowing what to do with it that counts.

For me, keeping track of time started at Rockhurst High School in Kansas City, where the Jesuits taught us to schedule our activities in precise Accountant segments. Here is what a page from the daily list I kept for four years looked like:

Wednesday, March 1, 1961

- 5:30 - up; prayers
- 5:31 - teeth; face
- 5:35 - shave
- 5:40 - dress, hair
- 5:45 - room
- 5:50 - Ms, clox; basket
- 5:55 - reading
- 6:10 - paper
- 6:20 - Mr C; Lee
- 7:00 - eat; clippings; read s.
- 7:30 - school; social; bull.
- 7:40 - books
- 7:45 - office
- 8:00 - class
  Study Hall
  Greek
  History
- 12:05 - Kali schol?; deadlines
  eat: social; office;
  read SM
- 1:00 - Study Hall
  Latin
  MM Maps
  Physics read bk. collate

- 2:40 - read
- 3:00 - AE
- 4:30 - home, mail; clippings;
  eat; social; paper, finances;
  exercise; Sat. walk; library
  MM, Eng., Lat; George; read
- 7:00 Reynolds
- 7:25 - services, mail
- 8:15 - read
- 8:30 - Broadmaur
- 9:30 - read; feet
- 10:40 - record; chart
- 10:45 - teeth, face. dress
- 10:50 - schedule
- 10:58 - Exam C; AC
- 11:00 - TAPS

Note that the end of my March 1 daily agenda, which was written in pencil, was tomorrow's to-do list: At 10:50 P.M. I allowed myself eight minutes to work on the next day's agenda. All day March 1, I'd been jotting down notes in pencil to remind myself of things that had to be scheduled for March 2. During the eight minutes at the end of March 1, I created the agenda for March 2. Note also that all but one of the individual items on the March 1 agenda are items of micromanagement (defined as what to do on the Accountant's clock when). The eight minutes at 10:50 P.M. are macromanagement— considerably less than 1 percent of the time available to me.

Though it served me well as a foundation for future productivity, I'm sure it's immediately obvious that an adult living at the start of the new millennium, in a life filled with interruptions and imme- diate demands, can't live sanely for long with this excessively disci- plined approach. But *accurate description precedes effective prescription*. For accurate consciousness of time usage to arise, you must take control one way or another. As years passed, I learned that I had to move on from the severe but satisfying monastic time-management methods of my Jesuit agendas. I experimented with macromanagement tech- niques—what I call "the Gordian knot style of time management": Cut through the busyness by doing the important matters first, and letting everything else take care of itself.

The most familiar macro tool is the to-do list. It's excellent for getting specific small objectives accomplished, but ultimately you'll want to move on because using the to-do list to control your life ends up wasting too much time. Yes, you get the important little things done. But you can't write, "Become an internationally rec- ognized architect" on your to-do list. The to-do list doesn't moti- vate or inspire you because it doesn't deal with goals and dreams, only with objectives. That's why even the shortest to-do list often gets neglected, ignored, postponed, constantly carried over from one day to the next. There's a rebellion going on inside you. Checking completed tasks off the list may satisfy your Accountant, but your Visionary is longing for more and feeling cheated.

I've developed two forms that can help you inventory your actual expenditure of time so that you can take charge of this most precious asset and attach it firmly to your dream plan— without becoming a Jesuit.

The Time Inventory Daily Worksheet should be filled out at the end of each day, estimating the number of hours you spend on the various activities in your life. The example that follows belongs to an imaginary man who wants to move from his day job as a bank teller to selling the nonfiction book he's writing.

TIME INVENTORY DAILY WORKSHEET
(IN HOURS)   WEEK OF _____

ACTIVITY	SUN.	MON.	TUES.	WED.	THURS.	FRI.	SAT.	TOTAL
Sleeping	8	8	6	7	9	8	10	56
Sales Calls	0	2	4	3	1	2	1	13
Exercise	1	1	2	0	0	1	1	6
Eating/Family	4	2	1	3	2	3	5	20
Reading	1	2	0	0	0	0	1	4
Hygiene	0.5	0.5	0.5	1	0.5	0.5	0.5	4
Proposals	1	2	2	2	1	4	1	13
Organizing	2	1	1	0	0	0	1	5
Driving— Errands	1	2	2	2	3	2	2	14
Socializing	5	1	2	1	4	5	8	26
Day Job	0	8	8	8	8	8	0	40
Total Hours	23.5	29.5	28.5	27	28.5	33.5	30.5	201

TIME INVENTORY DAILY WORKSHEET
(IN HOURS)   WEEK OF _____

ACTIVITY	SUN.	MON.	TUES.	WED.	THURS.	FRI.	SAT.	TOTAL
Sleeping								
Total Hours								

When you're filling out your own worksheet, don't forget housework, church and/or volunteer activities, phone time, and the like. If the categories here don't sound right to you, alter them to suit your own life and activities. Don't add up the totals beneath or to the right until the week is over. But at the end of the week, add them up. Our bank teller came up with 201 hours. Ninety percent of my students and clients end up with weekly audits far under or considerably over 168. What's magical about the number 168? The accountant is right about this one: 168 is exactly how many hours are in the week for all of us—whether you're the pope, an ice skater, the president of the United States, a stockbroker, a major league baseball player, a bank teller, or a hairdresser.

The discrepancy between your count and 168 arises because you are unaware of the interaction among the three voices within your mind. In his first week of keeping track, notice that our future published writer has recorded activities to fill 201 hours in the week. Where did the extra thirty-three hours come from? Now that he's admitted the discrepancy and recognized its magnitude, he's ready to get serious. Obviously, he's more careful using the worksheet the second week, making sure he keeps closer tabs on where the time is going.

Once you've used these worksheets for two weeks, you have an accurate enough idea of where your time is going to make use of the Actual Time Inventory Analysis Worksheet. Fill out the activity and hours-per-week columns using the results of your second Time Inventory Daily Worksheet.

ACTUAL TIME INVENTORY ANALYSIS WORKSHEET

ACTIVITY	HOURS PER WEEK	VISIONARY QUOTIENT (1–5)	ACCOUNTANT QUOTIENT (1–5)	MIND'S EYE TOTAL (1–10)
1 Sleeping	56	xxxxxxxxxx	xxxxxxxxxxxxx	xxxxxxxx
2 Day Job	40	0	5	5

continued...

ACTUAL TIME INVENTORY ANALYSIS WORKSHEET (continued)

ACTIVITY	HOURS PER WEEK	VISIONARY QUOTIENT (1–5)	ACCOUNTANT QUOTIENT (1–5)	MIND'S EYE TOTAL (1–10)
3 Eating/Family	14	2	3	5
4 Sales Calls	13	5	2	7
5 Insurance Classes	13	5	1	6
6 Exercise	6	5	3	8
7 Driving—Errands	12	1	1	2
8 Reading	2	3	1	4
9 Hygiene	2	1	2	3
10 Socializing	6	0	2	2
11 Organizing	4	4	0	4
Total Hours	168			

Now, we want to find out, on a scale of 1 to 5 (5 being the highest), how much each activity serves your dream goals. This is its Visionary Quotient. And we're not going to fool with sleeping because the right amount of sleep is essential on all fronts.

There's nothing magical about filling out the Visionary Quotient column. Follow your gut reaction.

The Accountant Quotient column rates the activity's importance to your physical, financial, and psychological welfare. Taking writing classes, as far as your Accountant's gut reaction is concerned, has minimal present value. Your paycheck from the bank is keeping the potatoes on the table. Obviously, on the other hand, this teller's Visionary hates his day job. But notice that neither his Visionary nor his Accountant is thrilled with the twelve hours weekly this man spends on errands. Although some writers might regard socializing as a valuable activity, our example doesn't. His Visionary hates it as much as he hates his day job, and his Accountant rates it only a 2.

If he's going to do anything about his socializing, he should think about socializing with different people (exchanging the coffee shop in his neighborhood for the one next door to the newspaper, where at least the social interaction might lead to useful networking).

The third column, presided over by your Mind's Eye, combines the two quotients. This man's bank job is a pain in the neck to his Visionary, but it does pay the bills—an activity the Accountant values to the utmost. It receives a 0 in the Visionary Quotient column, a 5 in the Accountant Quotient column. But your Mind's Eye acknowledges that any activity with a combined quotient of 5 or above will not be dropped or seriously reduced in time investment, thereby keeping both serpents happy.

The blank Actual Time Inventory Analysis Worksheet below is for your reassessment. Fill in the categories to suit your own life.

ACTUAL TIME INVENTORY ANALYSIS WORKSHEET

ACTIVITY	HOURS PER WEEK	VISIONARY QUOTIENT (1–5)	ACCOUNTANT QUOTIENT (1–5)	MIND'S EYE TOTAL (1–10)
1 Sleeping		xxxxxxxxxx	xxxxxxxxxxxxx	xxxxxxxx
2				
3				
4				
5				
6				
7				
8				
9				
10				
11				
Total Hours	168			

As it recognizes the unique power of both his Accountant's and his Visionary's perception of time, our teller's Mind's Eye knows that the yin of Accountant time and the yang of Visionary time are both valid, simultaneous, and equally important in their places and for their purposes. Telling them both that they're correct, and that they can take turns, his Mind's Eye negotiates with the Accountant to allow a conservative, cautious amount of time during which the success dreams of the Visionary can be explored. Without the Mind's Eye's intervention, he was constantly conflicted over his use of time. With his Mind's Eye's help and negotiation, he begins to steal time for success, using his Goal Time Worksheet to carve hours from the twenty-four-hour clock and to mine, methodically, the breakthrough energy of the Visionary.

GOAL TIME WORKSHEET

ACTIVITY	HOURS PER WEEK
1 Sleeping	56
2 Day Job	44
3 Eating/Family	11
4 Sales Calls	24
5 Insurance Classes	13
6 Exercise	6
7 Driving—Errands	2
8 Reading	2
9 Hygiene	2
10 Socializing	6
11 Organizing	2
Total Hours	168

GOAL TIME WORKSHEET

ACTIVITY	HOURS PER WEEK
1 Sleeping	
2 New Career	Stopwatch hours:
3	
4	
5	
6	
7	
8	
9	
10	
11	
Total Hours	168

Activities that rate less than a 5 in the M.E. column are subject to first-round negotiation. Let's say you hate doing yard work, and give it a 0 Visionary Quotient and a 1 Accountant Quotient. Obviously, we're going to find a way to get that particular activity out of your life. In our teller's inventory, "Driving/Errands" falls into this category. So he figures out a way of no longer doing errands. Instead of spending twelve hours a week on errands, he decides to do four hours of overtime at the bank to pay for someone to do the shuttle service for him. Or he moves closer to his day job. These revised decisions, which become "goals," are recorded in the Goal Time Worksheet. Notice that by reducing "Driving/Errands" to two hours, and making a few other adjustments, he's been able to increase "Sales Calls" from thirteen to twenty-four hours a week—which will inevitably advance his dream more quickly. At the same time, he's managed to increase the percentage of time devoted to the pursuit of his Type C dream from 16 percent (combining "Sales Calls," "Writing Classes," and "Reading") to 26 percent because he's increased the time available to make those sales calls, but he's also changed his way of socializing so that it serves the dream as well.

time to schedule time

No time you spend is more important than the time you spend scheduling your time; and that needn't be more than a tiny fraction of the time available to you. But scheduling your time is doomed to ineffectiveness unless you begin from the reality baseline of knowing what you've been doing with your time, and confronting your own lack of awareness about where your time has been going. The blank Goal Time Worksheet helps your Mind's Eye complete and memorialize its contract with Accountant and Visionary.

Once your knowledge of your time usage has allowed you to set new goals and objectives regarding the use of time, how in this busy, busy, busy world do you enforce the objectives for yourself? How can you schedule a life that is a long, endless, shrieking, demanding interruption? After all, you can only turn off the phone for so long without losing your illusion of control and all contact with reality.

how to make "the clock of life" your clock: the stopwatch

You know the clock on the wall will keep ticking away relentlessly until the day has gone by. You even know how it keeps ticking at night—why else would you awaken at 5:59 when you've set your digital bedside clock to go off at 6:00? You know the telephone seems wired to that damned clock, life's interruptions seem wired to it, the myriad distractions that flesh is heir to seem wired to it— and you recognize that, as a result, you yourself and your dreams have been wired to the Accountant's clock for way too long. Your world has been defined by that relentless, uncreative clock. You are desperate to realize your Goal Time.

Mercury's contemporary caduceus for taking command of your time is the stopwatch. Here's how to use that magic wand: I suggest buying the simplest one you can find, one that allows you to stop the seconds and restart them, without the other countless modes that will drive you crazy unless you're training racehorses. Hang the stopwatch above your computer, your telephone, your worktable—above whatever altar serves the god of your career transit dream. Promise yourself that, no matter what happens on that wall clock, you will work on your dream at least one hour before you go to bed tonight.

Or two hours. Try one first, then expand slowly and naturally in the direction of that Goal Time. Keep it as simple as you can and still make it work for you. Using the stopwatch allows me the illusion of freedom I value highly, but also ensures the constant sense of disciplined progress toward the success I've mapped out for myself. Nothing is more satisfyingly inevitable than the achievements that time creates from small, stolen increments. One hour a day is thirty hours a month. Thirty hours a month will inevitably produce results, especially if you've programmed the three parts of your mind effectively to make the best possible use of that hour. Imagine how quickly a writer marketing her work will move forward, having assigned five hours a week to marketing calls and letters. She realizes that the faster she gets through those Nos, the sooner she gets to the Yes. And it just takes time to get through the Nos.

If the one-hour-per-day approach doesn't work for your unpredictable schedule, or makes you feel too disciplined, make it a weekly approach. One of my workshop students was having trouble keeping to his contract that he'd put in two hours writing per day. After several give-and-takes, we came down to the real reason he was having problems: he was leaving his day job in order to be free, and the daily discipline we'd been discussing made him feel enslaved again. I asked him if he'd be comfortable committing to a *weekly* number of hours, to bringing in his stopwatch to the next session with ten hours on it.

"And I could do them in whatever configuration I choose?"

"Absolutely. The whole idea is to find a way of tricking your mind into allowing you to live by your own clock."

He came in the next week with 10:06 on his stopwatch, and the weeks after with 10:04, 9:56, 10:10. He'd found a way of using the caduceus to give him that necessary illusion of freedom and control combined with the satisfaction of real progress in committing hours to his career transit.

crisis management

I wrote *A Writer's Time* when I was still primarily a professor, following a schedule that was generally set by the college catalogue a year in advance. In the years since, the challenges to my time- and work-management needs and techniques became more and more unfamiliar. At the point when I had two films shooting simultaneously, two in preproduction, and four in postproduction, every morsel of time was an occasion for what medical people call "triage." What do I do at this moment that will do the greatest good, or at least the least damage, to the overall project? My phone had five lines, all of which were lit up nearly twelve hours a day. How do you choose which line to pick up when each call is from a different director who is either being interviewed, in preproduction, in production, and in postproduction—and the other line is the financier? How do you steal time to pull over to the curb and figure this one out?

When the first crisis occurred, I was convinced that "We don't have *time* for crises." But that conviction soon disintegrated as crisis after crisis came along. Finally, I realized that "We have to *make time* for crises." I asked my assistant to "time" the next crisis. Over a period of two weeks, we learned that, on average, one crisis occurred each day, at unpredictable intervals. But, to my delight, the average time for getting through the crisis and going on with our crazy routine was under an hour. Crises seem much more demanding to the Accountant's imagination; but by enlisting the Mind's Eye's help in timing them, the truth was revealed: There was something predictable about them. The Accountant needs the help of the Mind's Eye to put crises in perspective. Mercury's caduceus comes to his aid to realize that even crises can be managed by arranging to steal time for them. We began scheduling "throwaway" activities so that at least two throwaways were scheduled each day instead of being clumped into a slow day. That way, when a crisis occurred, we could immediately implement the alternate plan for the throwaway activity. For example, I liked to be at wardrobe fittings for the leads; if a crisis occurred, I sent my assistant, with a Polaroid, instead.

don't forget that only you can call "time out!"

anonymous: It's not over 'til the fat lady sings.
atchity: It's not over, but you can call time out.

I used to wish I could call "Time out!" to give myself time to regroup and figure out the meaning of life. I used to fantasize about building in an extra, dateless, hourless day each week to give us time off: no appointments, no phone calls, no deadlines. But that is daydreaming, undisciplined Visionary thinking; we are trapped in an Accountant's world.

You can get time out on a regular basis by stealing it. Now that you've embraced your career transit and are living the entrepreneurial life, don't forget to give yourself the benefits that your day job employer was forced to give you. Sometimes we are so excited about doing the things we love on a daily basis that we forget to give ourselves a break from them. "I don't need a vacation. My life is a vacation!"

Everyone needs vacations. Most people need them because work is exhausting. The entrepreneur needs them because vacations bring perspective and creative insights that are unavailable under the daily pressures of the career transit. "To do great work," Samuel Butler wrote, a person "must be very idle as well as very industrious." The entrepreneur, as both employer and employed, must schedule his vacations, with alternate dates in mind in case "something comes up" that forces a change. You are accomplishing just as much if not more when you get away from the whistle and allow your mind to play.

Vacations for the entrepreneur are excursions into Visionary time. Getaway time, like the aboriginal Dreamtime, puts your

Mind's Eye in direct touch with the Visionary's view of what you've been doing on a daily basis, and what you could be doing more creatively. Traveling away from Base 1 is always good for the entrepreneur because it causes a cross-pollinating effect among your objectives, goals, and projects. Traveling anywhere away from a project is a kind of vacation, and nearly always offers a creative advantage; but traveling should be distinguished from true vacations. Going to New York on business, or going home to see your family for a week, are vacations that can bring fresh perspective. But in both cases there are too many things to do for the most constructive form of abandonment to occur. A true vacation is being on the island of Maui, where, after a couple of days of readjustment to "heavenly Hana," your to-do list consists of two items, and you somehow never quite get around either to doing them or to caring that you didn't. You notice suddenly that the days seem long, immense; that time has become, as Jorge Luis Borges puts it, "like a plaza." Smaller getaways can produce the same effect: mountain hiking; wandering through the museum; deep-sea fishing for a day; just hanging out at Grand Central Station or at the Plaza Oak Bar watching the world go by. During a true vacation Mercury can bring you an Olympian perspective, where the patterns of your life and activities become apparent among the tangle of busyness.

It is precisely at such times that the entrepreneur's creative process falls prey to chaos theory. Chaos theory posits the all-important impact of tiny, random events on the long-range prediction of physical cycles. Weather patterns could be predicted accurately were it not for the "butterfly effect": Somewhere a Monarch butterfly fluttering from flower to flower (an incident too small to measure) minutely disrupts the passage of the breeze, and a thousand miles away a middle-sized storm turns into a tornado. Chaos theory is the despair of Accountants, who spend their lives trying to predict patterns, as though chaos didn't exist. But to the Visionary, chaos is the staff of Mercury. The German philosopher Friedrich Nietzsche, in *Thus Spake Zarathustra*, his most Visionary work, wrote: "One must still have chaos in one to give birth to a dancing star."

The entrepreneur arranges his true vacations to put him in direct touch with chaos, following winding roads to heavenly dream places inaccessible to ordinary travelers. The following are tips on time and work management:

- *Rate everything that crosses your desk 1, 2, or 3.* Then make an agenda for the 1s immediately, and immediately delegate the 2s to someone else. Put the 3s in a drawer designated the "3-drawer," setting aside a few hours once a month to go through it and see what's still important enough to deal with. You'll discover that most of the contents of the 3-drawer are even less important now than they were originally. Napoleon supposedly had all his mail dumped before the bags were opened, on the premise that the important news would have reached him already and anything he neglected that should not have been neglected would make itself known. I'm sure that Josephine quickly found an alternative method of communicating with her emperor.
- *Postpone procrastination!* Anthony Robbins says, "The best way to deal with procrastination is to postpone it." Procrastinate with everything except your dream. To make that happen you need to. . .
- *Solve each problem as it occurs, as much as possible.* Postponing the solution automatically increases the total amount of time needed for it. Opening a letter, then stacking it somewhere, is counterproductive. If you know from the envelope that the letter isn't important, toss it in the nearest wastebasket and don't even take it into your den.

selective pruning

mencius: Men must be decided on what they will not do, and then they are able to act with vigor in what they ought to do.

atchity: Don't do what you can do. Do what only *you* can do.

Just as the vitality of a tree can work against the tree unless the
experienced arboriculturist prunes the weaker branches, dreams
can be dangerous unless you understand their peculiar fertility.
Work creates more work, and one dream breeds another, usually
grander than the one before. Success has ramifications, breeding all
kinds of activities; and, unless you recognize that and infuse
regrouping time into your success agenda, you'll suddenly find
yourself too busy to be successful again.

well-meaning friend: You're such an enthusiast.
atchity: Why does that sound like an accusation?

Enthusiasts must protect themselves from their enthusiasms. To
accomplish this, I suggest the following:

- **Hold a monthly "drop" meeting with yourself.** The
  object of the meeting is to select activities that can be
  dropped for a month, with a promise to reevaluate their
  importance at your next meeting. I go through my
  project files monthly and force myself to table or discard
  the weaker ones, thereby constantly improving the quality
  of the projects I work on. As you become experienced in
  the Type C life, you'll recognize that one of its strangest
  characteristics is the necessity of killing the little monsters
  that once were bright dreams nipping at your heels. The
  smaller dreams must now be pruned away so that the
  bigger ones can thrive. Of course, it's even better to kill
  them off before they begin to grow. As Albert Camus
  said, "It's better to resist at the beginning than at the end."
- **Don't feel bad about the discards.** Celebrate them.
  More than sacrifices or disappointments, they are symptoms of your disciplined progress. Just because you can do
  something, after all, no longer means that you must or
  should do it. That was the old you, dominated by the
  Accountant, before your Mind's Eye opened to engage
  you in an entrepreneurial career transit.

- **When evaluating new projects, keep in mind the sign that psychoanalyst Carl Jung had framed above his desk**: Yes ~~No Maybe~~ is crossed out as well as 'No" to remind us that it's the "Maybes" that devour our time and dream energies. If the answer to an incoming idea or request isn't definitively "Yes," it's definitively "No." Never Maybe. "Maybe" kills countless ambitions and splendid plans. "We are what we pretend to be," says Kurt Vonnegut's narrator in *Mother Night*, "so we must be careful about what we pretend to be." You may also find it useful to go through the following checklist:

  - *Is this a good idea (or opportunity)?* Yes or No.
  - *Is this idea directly connected with my dream?* Yes or No. If the answer is No, pass it along to someone else with no strings attached.
  - *Does this idea fit into my present agenda?* If not, is it such a good idea that I should revise my agenda to accommodate it?
  - *Is the world ready for this idea?*
  - *Am I ready to spend years bringing it to fruition?*

It's extremely important to consider both internal and external timing when it comes to evaluating new ideas and opportunities. Many of us waste time on good ideas whose time has either come and gone or won't be coming for too long a time to make its present implementation productive. Of course, thanks to the predictably unpredictable impact of chaos on our lives, we can never be certain about timing. But we can be certain about our gut reaction to the checklist.

> So long as you live, be radiant, and do not grieve at all. Life's span is short and time exacts the final reckoning.
> —Epitaph of Seikilos for his wife (100 B.C.)

6

a day in the type c life

annie: The sun'll come out tomorrow!
atchity: Meanwhile how do we make it through today?

One night, walking up to my front door, I felt like I was walking on air. I had experienced such a good day I felt I'd died and gone to heaven. I'd gotten up before dawn to write for three hours, closing in on the end of a new screenplay. Then I'd spent an hour exercising and reading a motivational book. After getting dressed, I went back to my desk and made phone calls—one of them to an agent who was thrilled to accept a client's novel for representation. In the mail I discovered that one of my own books had been accepted for publication and I received a letter out of the blue from a professor who'd read my most recent essay and was inviting me to speak at Villanova and Bryn Mawr.

At lunch, I made a new financing contact who assured me he'd get in touch with the person in charge of raising money for my next project. The afternoon had brought me the first meeting with an exciting new writing client and agreement on casting with a finance company for a film about to go into preproduction. An early dinner with my best friend was followed by the last meeting of my workshop, where everyone thanked me for the past eight productive and happy sessions. Suddenly, I had a vision of an angry goddess coming around the corner and blasting me with a shotgun. And I realized I would have greeted death with a laugh. In such a good mood, and in the middle of my dream, what better way to go?

That was a good day.

the waiting room

eliza: Just you wait, Henry Higgins, just you wait.
atchity: I don't mind waiting if I have good work to do while
I wait.

Most days are neither good nor bad. They're a mixture—bringing as many moments of step-by-step progress as moments of new obstacles and aggravations. Getting through ordinary days is the true test of stamina, because their endlessness is exhausting. I call these ordinary days the "waiting room," because so much of the time the career transit hero is waiting for that new career to take off.

At first, with your initial burst of energy, you try to turn the waiting room into the emergency room. Picking up the pressure, you think, will expedite the process. Sooner or later you'll learn that this approach produces diminishing returns. Most of the time, you simply have to wait. And waiting can be a real pain, though, as William Lynch reminds us, "The ability to wait is central to hope."

I've noticed over the years that I've formed what might be called a waiting pattern, with the underlying theme of "Work while you wait."

breakfasting on hope

lewis carroll: All the king's horses and all the king's
men/Couldn't put Humpty together again.
atchity: Never try to get your head together before you've
found all the pieces.

Until my new career became successful, my day began with moti-
vating myself to get out of bed in the morning. I'd noticed that
once I'd actually gotten my feet on the floor, the day seemed
bearable. But dragging myself from the blankets could be a task
that required Mercury's guidance to accomplish. Those who
embrace the dream quest know that the first important move of
the morning is "getting your head together." You can do it in bed;
you can do it while the coffee is brewing, or while you're having
your cup of tea. Some do it walking, jogging, or exercising. Others
prefer meditation or staring out the window.

Getting your head together, one way or the other, is a visualization technique: concentrating your inner vision on the potential
positives of the day ahead so you can translate them into action
that will inevitably, sooner or later, produce results. You'll decide
how and when you'll focus today's ration of creative energy. If the
day looks particularly forbidding, you'll decide how you'll protect
that energy from the cruel world, remembering that you are its
sole arbiter and protector. To fail to take the time in the morning
to make those crucial decisions is to dishonor the dream world.
Benjamin Disraeli said, "We make our fortunes and call them
fate." You must put yourself in charge of how you see the day
ahead. "The fault, dear Brutus," as Shakespeare's Cassius points out
in *Julius Caesar*, "is not in our stars, but in ourselves."

The Type C's day begins properly when he has designed it to
his own purposes. I could always tell how successfully my Mind's
Eye was functioning by the length of time it took me to rebuild
my head in the morning. If I bounded out of bed, it was because
the dream world was so close to becoming a reality that even my
Accountant could sense it. If the process took half an hour, I knew
my Mind's Eye had to work overtime to convince the grumbling
Accountant and the wounded Visionary that the good times
would indeed someday roll.

Mercury's inspiration means focusing on your hopes for the
day, allowing the patron god of Type Cs to escort your weary soul
into your chosen battle. I center my day in various ways,

depending on what I imagine it might bring. If the day's hope was that a decision might occur that I'd been waiting for, or a check might arrive that was long overdue, I centered myself by figuring out a way to protect that hope. If I was supposed to call for the decision, I would decide to call at 4:00 P.M., not at 9:00 A.M., so that I could have a good day in the meantime, either way. I also decided that, regardless of what I learned at four, I would do something pleasurable at five: take in a film, go for a walk with a friend, invite a favorite client or associate for a Cajun dinner. Planning for an enchanted evening always gives me something to look forward to. With that in mind, I can make it through anything.

If I could see no hope at all on the day's horizon, I'd do my best to manufacture some. For me, this often meant taking all the phones off the hook to spend the day writing, with my back to the world. I've noticed that doing this generally produced two benefits: First, I felt great about myself after a day of solid creative endeavor; and second, the world seemed somehow to feel bad about being such a deterrent to my dream, and almost always had something hopeful to report the moment I switched it back online.

At the worst extreme, I forced myself to leave the house and go off for a cup of coffee in a public place like L.A.'s Farmers Market. I reminded myself that the world I live in is the world I'd chosen for myself and designed. It didn't take long for my psychic energies to regenerate when I compared my situation to those I imagined of the circumstances of passersby. I recognized that I preferred my lifestyle to that of the nonweird. I also reminded myself that it was not necessary to see a happy conclusion to my whole life—it was enough simply to visualize making it through the day with my hope and vision intact. Creative intensity demanded that, as much as possible, I remain intent in and on the present. Finally, I reminded myself that by focusing on my work, whatever happened, I would leave less time for worry. Some people recommend smiling at yourself in the bathroom mirror. I recommend singing—in the shower, in the rain, or otherwise.

I used to keep a sign posted inside the medicine cabinet: "Yesterday hero: Today superhero." It psyched me up for the battles of the day by reminding me that I'd heroically overcome yesterday's obstacles. It gave me something to sing about.

good morning: vision and salesmanship

The best morning is the morning you move another step forward toward your goal, at the height of your enthusiasm. I would schedule new sales calls for the morning, or work on my own writing project. What these activities have in common is that they are more, rather than less, under my control, whereas actions that are already part of a project in progress are tied to forces beyond my control. A typical morning is getting up at 4:00 to hit my writing desk by 4:30. I'll write until 6:00 or 6:30, and then begin making marketing calls, first to New York (before they go to lunch), then elsewhere. As much as possible, I try to follow up each call immediately. If someone wants to see a screenplay or a book, I dictate the cover letter and arrange to get it on its way before making the next call.

This is prime outreach time. Because I've noticed that my belief in myself is always strongest at the moment of initial contact with a new associate, I initiate in the morning, putting my belief into action. Give yourself a limited number of high priority new sales calls to make each day and you'll see your action produce results. Worst case, you'll be getting through that finite list of "Nos" as quickly as possible—remembering your determination to turn each of them into a future "Nos."

At 7:30 I usually go off to the gym or the tennis courts for an hour and a half, to return around 9:00 to begin calling and meeting on Pacific Time.

When you believe in yourself and/or your project, your vision becomes contagious—assuming you either have, or can fake, the self-confidence required to follow through. Success comes from making other people see what you see. In ancient times it was generally a seer or a prophet who sold society on what it should value most highly. Your objective on each sales call is to create the lens through which the prospect views what you're selling. Never allow cold readings. If you can't create a positive lens, focus on creating a neutral one by seeking an open-minded consideration.

Keep in mind, no matter how pressured you are emotionally or financially, a long-term relationship with your buyer is more valuable to your dream than an immediate sale. (Your buyer is not responsible for your present needs, much less for past problems.) The right network for you will be one of mutual respect; where your buyer respects your product even if it doesn't fit her needs at the moment, and you respect your buyer's needs. Never, or at least rarely, try to sell her something that doesn't fit her market. Listen to your prospect. Pull back the moment you sense a negative decision, and begin working instead on the future of the relationship.

I've discovered that a sales call works best for me when I couch it as an information call. I'm calling to inform someone about a product and to ask his advice on its market; to inform myself about the market, as seen through the eyes of this particular buyer. Couching a call this way always allows me to enjoy it and to make it a positive, hopeful experience.

no one can reject you but yourself!

anonymous: A prophet is rejected in his own country.
atchity: True prophets reject rejection.

Of course you can't avoid hearing the word "No." If it's true that you can't fail at being yourself, why does the "No" word hurt so much of the time? Because you're just not good at being yourself yet. You've got to fall in love with "No," learn to see it as a come-on, an enticement, a challenge. One way or another, you must deal with "No" to suit your own purposes, find the chink in its armor.

Some writers burn their rejection slips. Others have more scatological approaches—like the German composer, who wrote to a critic: "I am sitting in the smallest room in my house. I have your criticism in front of me. Soon it will be behind me." At the outset of my freelance writing career, I papered the bathroom wall with the worst of my rejection slips. My father came to California for a visit. I hadn't told him about the guest bathroom. When he went to use it in the middle of a dinner party, he returned to the table with a long face. "What's wrong, Dad?" I asked.

"That bathroom," he said. "I'm really proud of you." Then, after a few minutes had passed, he added, "God, that's depressing."

I learned more about my father's conservative nature that night. He didn't like to be rejected and had constructed a life for himself in which little rejection could occur. I didn't like rejection either, but was trying to master it. At first by blatant confrontation, but gradually by redefining all these "Nos" as steps forward.

Whatever your approach, coming to terms with rejection is an absolutely inevitable early stage of Type C success. Thomas Edison said, "He who's never made a mistake has never made anything." The sooner you're rejected, the sooner you'll be accepted. Think about it. If what you're proposing weren't creative, original, and unique, everyone would say "Yes" immediately. You're doing something new, so rejection is predictable. And if they're telling you "No!" they're the wrong people for you. Do you want the wrong person to say "Yes"? Enormous time can be wasted when the wrong people say "Yes." Not only do you need a "Yes," you need a "Yes" from the right person.

As you become more accustomed to rejection, you learn to transform each "No" into a linkage. Each conversation that is less than a definite "Yes" becomes a definite "Maybe" because you accept the buyer's needs and because you don't associate his present, temporary rejection of your product with a judgment about you.

Don't be quick to conclude that a negative response is a rejection. Keep in mind that everyone is saddled with lack of self-confidence, including your prospective buyer. A negative initial response can often be turned around by your insistence, with all due respect, that the buyer doesn't understand the value of the product you're offering and you'd like a chance to demonstrate.

Often your excitement, when you believe in it enough to press it, will open the buyer's mind to seeing the product your way. Even if you've had a dozen negative responses in a row, and you're beginning to think all the odds are against you, don't let your current discouragement turn into pessimism. Optimism is still the only policy that makes logical sense. The truly great salespeople base their success not on what they've sold but on the act of selling. They love it. Even after they've made millions, they can't stay away from that door behind which another "Yes," a challenging "No," or a definite "Maybe" may be lurking.

doing lunch

In my line of work, lunches are so traditional that it took me years to realize that they aren't necessary much of the time. I've also discovered that few people are offended if I try to conduct the same business, or even the get-acquainted conversation, over the telephone, which is an enormous timesaver. I've reduced my business Los Angeles lunches from an average of four a week to one or two a week. I've also learned to replace lunch with a walk. I schedule my management and consulting clients between twelve and three because I know everyone else in town is at lunch during those hours. Or I'll schedule a late-afternoon drink instead of lunch, so that I can spend the lunch hour on the phone with New York (before they leave for the day), or catching up my desk (with the side benefit of not ruining my diet from too much restaurant food). The point is always to design your day around your purposes, finding new ways to advance your dream.

"how softly runs the afternoon"

Before management and production became all consuming, the afternoon was a time for me to wind down and lessen stress. After spending an hour on follow-up calls after lunch, I would try to find quiet activity to carry me to dinnertime. This was a great time for errands, for catching a film, reading, going for a drive, taking a walk, or taking a nap. From 3:00 to 4:00 P.M. I was on the phone, from 4:00 to 5:00 trying to find that quiet time. When I did, I'd realize that the hours of 5:00 to 7:00 were highly productive—usually receiving phone calls from people who'd waited until the end of the day to deal with a project. So from 5:00 to 7:00 I'd schedule activities at my desk that could bear interrupting (letter writing, accounting, organizing, making notes on tomorrow's marketing calls). And I was happy to be interrupted by the phone.

enchanted evening

cajun proverb: There's always something to celebrate.
atchity: Celebrate making it through the day.

You're not going to have a terrible day if you've planned a pleasurable evening. That's why planning the evening is one of the most effective methods of centering yourself in the morning. Make the evening a time to celebrate, to entertain friends, to retreat, to go bar hopping, to roam around, hang out with friends or family, to play "Guts," to enjoy the fact that you're alive, to abandon the hunt and take your daily vacation from the intensity of your life. I have to force myself away from the desk sometimes in order to put this into practice, and I don't always succeed because my desk is usually overflowing and I love my work. But I find the evening most pleasurable when things didn't go as smoothly as I would've liked them to during the day. If the evening has been enchanted, your dreams will be sweet dreams— the best possible preparation for a bright tomorrow.

7

money mania

jack benny: I never said money was the most important thing in life. . . . It's just a heck of a long ways ahead of whatever's in second place.
accountant: You're living beyond your means.
visionary: Then get your ass in gear, and increase our means.
cajun saying: You know you're still alive if it's costing you money.

Time and money are the lifeblood of dreams. Yet we live in a society where, according to some, it's more painful to speak personally about money than about sex. The American Accountant is especially strong because of our pervasive Puritan heritage, our national love affair with practicality and immediate security.

Tom Bergin used to write to me encouragingly, "Don't worry about money. Money always comes." I used to find it exceedingly difficult to trust this advice, thanks to my accountant father and money-conscious family. But I've found that it's true. Somehow there always seems to be enough for what's important. "You will find a way to 'access' what's required," as another mentor, Linda Levinson, once told me. Money does grow on trees. The money tree is the fertile, well-managed garden of your mind. Someone once chided me, "You think money comes out of a faucet, endlessly," and I replied: "Doesn't it?" Consider Walt Disney's attitude toward money:

> I've always been bored with making money . . . . I wanted to do things, I wanted to build things. Get something going. People look at me in different ways. Some of them say, "The guy has no regard for money." That is not true. I have had regard for money. But I'm not like some people who worship money as something you've got to have piled up in a big pile somewhere. I've only thought of money in one way, and that is to do something with it, you see? I don't think there is a thing that I own that I will ever get the benefit of, except through doing things with it.

Herb Goldberg and Robert T. Lewis, in their fascinating book *Money Madness*, offer a corollary: "When the satisfaction in having money submerges the satisfaction derived from the process of making money—then it can be said that the person has an unhealthy attachment to money."

Early in my career change I visited the father of one of my Occidental College students, a semiretired Prussian immigrant who had done well in the "new country" as a manufacturer. I'll never forget what he told me about America. "There's no reason," he said, "to fear failure in this country. There's no penalty for failure." When I asked him what he meant, he explained bankruptcy to me.

Growing up, I'd heard the word on more than one occasion. My father had undergone a severe midlife crisis of his own after the Pabst Blue Ribbon distributor for which he'd worked for twenty-five years suddenly went bankrupt. But before that, I'd always heard the word only in reference to my grandfather Atchity (we called him "Jede," and the one thing I remember him saying was "I hate stoplights!"). Jede, an immigrant from the "old country" of Lebanon, had gone bankrupt in America more than once. When World War II erupted, he'd just opened a candy factory and ordered a trainload of sugar for which he'd agree to pay twenty-two cents a pound. By the time the train pulled into Kansas City, the price of sugar had fallen to fifteen cents a pound. He'd also gone bankrupt when he invented a sanitary napkin he called Motex, then was undercut by Johnson & Johnson, who came out with Kotex priced "two for the price of one" until Jede's company bit the dust.

Yet by the time my grandfather died, he had amassed a sizable estate, enough to be proud of—especially considering that he'd raised a family of seven. I remember him as an energetic man, who knew how to relax with his music and laughter, but who, like my mother, always urged me to "go for it." He was the one who supported me when I decided, standing in the freshman registration line at Georgetown, to register for classics instead of pre-med. My father had a hard time with the phone call I had waited three weeks to make. "What are you going to do for a living?" he said. But Jede was proud of my decision and never doubted that I would someday become a distinguished professor.

Society hadn't penalized him for failing. It had encouraged him to succeed by allowing him to survive financial catastrophes through bankruptcy. Yes, you may have trouble with credit. But entrepreneurs always find a way, and "money talks." You can have zero credit and, when you have sufficient cash for a substantial down payment, buy whatever you need or want to buy—on "time."

It's a question of perspective, what you're willing to sacrifice and how you choose to see yourself.

At one point three years into my career change, after Lorimar went bankrupt, I was left in a disastrous financial position—suddenly overextended and personally at risk. Overnight, my prospects of income were reduced from a minimum of $250,000 per year to zero. With only three years' business experience, and having spent most of my time in Montreal for the period of the films' production, I had made no provisions for this Los Angeles corporation's bankruptcy. I returned to Los Angeles and struggled to keep my production company from drowning, facing personal bankruptcy every single week for the next six years. I had to sell my company, L/A House, because the money it was owed by distributors was so far in the future as to be irrelevant to my present. I had mistakenly associated my dream with L/A House, and had put all my eggs into its one basket.

With the help of my best friend and my trusted legal adviser, I recognized that the dream wasn't dead. It was still alive, although wounded and whimpering, within me. They taught me to associate the dream only with my own identity, so that flags, if necessary, can be left behind on the battlefield and the campaign can proceed. At the same time, I was going through the psychologically painful transition in loyalties—I was struggling to learn the television business—where cash flow is either extraordinary or laughable. When I came out the other end, and started my new company, Atchity Entertainment International (AEI), I made sure it was well diversified—books, films, television, Internet, and merchandising.

In the midst of my struggles, my father was diagnosed with cancer and given six months to live. He fought the diagnosis bravely and lived another two years so that he, an Accountant to the end, could make sure he'd put all his affairs in order. At one point, when I was visiting him in Kansas City, he gave me the blessing many a son waits a lifetime for in vain. He told me I had always been a good son; that he knew I'd achieve what I wanted to achieve, but that in the meantime I should declare personal bankruptcy and get on with my life.

His words lifted an immense burden from my shoulders. Not that I declared bankruptcy—I managed to hold it at bay while paying off the debts, through some of the "hooks and crooks" described below. But I gave myself permission to use bankruptcy, that perfectly legal and increasingly acceptable instrument of American society, if I had no alternative. Before, I had assumed I'd be in disgrace, with society and especially with my father, if I repeated his father's pattern. But my father had always been a fair man, and he was determining fairly that I'd made my best effort to recover and shouldn't continue making efforts that were counterproductive to my future potential.

One of the businesspeople I interviewed for this book describes himself as a "serial entrepreneur" and is presently CEO of a growing music and entertainment company. He was involved in raising capital for a multimedia (Internet plus television) interactive game, and made the mistake (recognized as such, of course, only in retrospect) of pursuing partnerships with entertainment agencies, studios, and broadcasters, thinking they were obvious sources for strategic capital. He and his partners put on a roadshow that gleaned great feedback from the target companies. "But we failed to realize we were only a speck on their radar," he said, adding that deal discussions slowly got nowhere. Term sheets, when they finally arrived, "did not reflect the discussions."

He and his partners returned to Toronto very disappointed, upset with themselves for having invested so much time in pursuit with zero results. He sat and waited by the phone for something to happen, but it just didn't—a much worse situation than if the project had gone nowhere from the beginning. The entire experience was one of his darkest hours as an entrepreneur.

But when I asked him what his darkest fear was during this darkest hour, I was surprised to discover it had nothing to do directly with not having enough money:

> My darkest fear was facing the possibility that I wouldn't achieve greatness. I wasn't worried about anything short-term, like not making it day-to-day or month-to-month. Most great entrepreneurs don't focus too much on those things. It was more the possibility that this could be that one idea that slipped by. The possibility that it wouldn't work was too much to handle. It led to a real identity crisis, a crisis of self-confidence.

I asked him how he was able to move from that crisis forward to continue pursuing his dream:

> It probably came down to blind faith and persistence, almost to the point of being unrealistic. No one ever contemplated abandoning the project. This blind dogmatic

belief that it was going to go somewhere got us back up on our feet. If there was even a snippet of a possibility in the wind, we jumped on it like wild savages; brought in every last thing we felt would contribute to the development of the company. Ultimately, that put us into a position where we were serendipitous—we stumbled into an acquisition of another company that became a money machine that financed the primary company. If we hadn't persisted through the darkness, we wouldn't have been there when the opportunity presented itself.

Q: What did you learn in retrospect?

A: The CEO of a major telecommunications company in Canada gave a speech about the benefits of persistence. You're going to go through dark moments, he said. You can count on it. Persistence isn't the only solution at times like this, but it is an order-qualifier. Without it you are guaranteed to fail. You've gotta get through those dark hours and believe you're going to make it. It doesn't mean you're going to succeed. Definitely you need some luck as well. My personal belief is that your situation will dictate how persistent you can be. It's a relative discussion. Robert Mondavi started his operation when he was in his late sixties or seventies. I would go to the ends of the earth for something I believe in because I'm that confident and that willing to take on the risk. The more reluctant you are to throw in the towel, the more likely you are to succeed.

Q: What advice would you give people from your experience?

A: Any venture needs to combine a few key elements: research, intelligence, learning, persistence, and knowing that there are never any guarantees of success. A business venture should never be approached in a half-assed way. The ability to put yourself into the mindset of everyone you have to deal with in order to succeed is crucial. I've seen, in cases of failure, massive inability on the part of the people at the heart of a new venture to put themselves into the mind of those who could make them succeed. Dedicating yourself to knowing the needs of the clients and buyers and vendors you're dealing with will come across on the surface level in a sales pitch. In general, it's your responsibility to come up with the most comprehensive gameplan you possibly can. What it takes for your new business to succeed, what happens if it doesn't succeed. Areas that can't be controlled have to be considered. All this will make you much stronger, and give you a real shot at success.

living on the edge
accountant: You like living on the edge, don't you?
atchity: Yes—and I'm also okay with admitting it.

I was telling another entrepreneur friend in New York that the edge is always wider than you imagine. He disagreed. "It's narrower than you imagine," he said. "But the longer you live on it, the wider it can get. At ten years, you can widen it yourself."

My widening formula goes this way: I'll do anything short of bankruptcy to stay afloat, including negotiating with bank creditors for payment extensions. I realized that my crisis was their crisis as well, and that they had a stake in my recovery. If they didn't cooperate, their alternative was my bankruptcy.

As I put this plan into action, I discovered that living on the edge was indeed a much wider existence than I'd previously imagined. I had seen bill-paying days, the first and fifteenth of the month (and I hated short months), basically as the end of the world. Bad attitude! I've since learned to see them as turning points and challenges, and I feel an immense satisfaction after I send out all the checks I can afford to send out and shuffle the papers in the "First" or "Fifteenth" files to hold over until the next period.

But when I wasn't able to make the institutional payments on the assigned date, I realized that nothing life-threatening happened.

Of course I'd always known that. Everyone has overlooked a payment and received a gentle reminder. In fact, we sometimes receive these gentle computer reminders even when we don't overlook a payment, with their last line, "If payment has already been sent, please disregard this notice." It's important to fully recognize that these reminders come from computers. If lack of funds is undermining your self-image on a given day, it may help you to realize that it's not an angry father or an angry god who's slapping your hands. It's a mechanically efficient, temperature-controlled computer.

Humans do get involved later. But when they do, their focus is entirely on your plans to pay. "When can we expect a payment?" They negotiate, they listen, they give advice. They only get angry when you ignore them. Not to experience all the stages of the process is to deprive yourself of an invaluable course in business reality. As someone who'd dutifully paid everything on time through all the years of my academic career, I was living in a magical kingdom with an unrealistic view of the actual edge and my degree of freedom.

Now, thanks to my challenging difficulties, I know I have much more maneuvering room than I'd thought. This gives me greater self-confidence. No one wants me to declare bankruptcy. I was the only person who had been holding a gun to my head.

do what you love

People are divided into those who go to work to earn a living and those whose work earns a living for them. The people in the first group, probably accounting for 95 percent of the human race, are security conscious, trapped, and perennially bored. Those in the second group, the Type Cs like you, have exchanged boredom for terror—but, in finding their vocation, have found the strength to deal with terror. Given the choice, they would much rather cling to their present terror than return to the security of boredom.

In the midst of the crisis involving my first company, I asked myself a hundred times a week if I'd made a terrible mistake leaving the serenity, respectability, and security of Occidental College. It got to a point where I couldn't tell which onboard voice was asking the question: the anxious Accountant, the crazy Visionary, or the disappointed and ready-to-concede-defeat Mind's Eye. After one particularly painful day, one of my beleaguered entrepreneur friends had tried to explain to me how much he valued his weekends at Army Reserve camp where he got to wear a uniform that everyone automatically respected instead of walking around naked in the jungle. I realized that I, too, sometimes missed the uniform I used to loathe. It had been, I thought I recalled, so comforting to belong to a social group that received automatic respect.

Things got so bad once that I drove to the Occidental campus around midnight and sat on a bench in the Spanish neoclassical quad, surrounded by Oxy's famous roses (now gone, by the way). It was a strange experience—my own little agony in the rose garden—for the first few moments, as I breathed in all I had given up. But I hadn't been sitting there for more than five minutes when the familiarity of my former life swept over me. The sensation was unmistakable: the palpable sensation of suffocation—including the sense of being left behind by the real world—that had prompted me to make the exit decision in the first place. It had taken me nearly a year, after receiving tenure, to identify that feeling. But I recognized it immediately when it returned to me that night.

As I drove home, feeling much better now that the voices were sorted out (the Accountant had been the culprit, as might have been predicted), I realized that I'd just tested for myself what my best friend had been telling me consistently: "You made the right decision." He'd also added: "Don't be a baby. You've been spoiled as a professor, and now you're in the real world with the big boys." On the drive home I recalled the sensation that night on the flight through the blizzard from Montreal to Toronto, when I wasn't the least bit worried about the zero visibility and turbulence because I knew that if I died then I'd be dying in the middle of my own dream. I was doing what I love to do. Leonardo da Vinci put it this way: "As a well spent day brings happy sleep, so life, well used, brings happy death."

My grandfather had always said to me, "Do what you love to do. Don't worry about the money." I advise my undergraduate and graduate students, as well as my clients, "Find whatever it is that makes you happiest, then figure out how to make a living doing it." When I was happy teaching, I couldn't believe people were paying me to do what I would have done for nothing. To be paid to do dream work is what we're all aiming for. My son, back from Salamanca for a visit, told me at lunch one day that he'd decided to move to Madrid and find a job. Remembering my advice, he'd figured out that being in Spain made him happiest, so he would live where he could get paid for loving Spain and being fluent in Spanish language and culture. I told him it was an excellent plan.

the comfort horizon
My *goal* had been a comfort horizon of three years—by which I mean a situation in which I could clearly see income for that period of time, allowing me more energy for purely creative endeavors (as opposed to financial survival efforts). My *objective* was a comfort horizon of six months, which would allow me to catch my breath. I've frequently reached my objective, requiring constant re-achievement, but the nice thing about it is that, after years of such achievements, I began to feel a new level of self-confidence. I didn't have to reduce my expenditures to make the paydays, choosing instead to maintain and increase my income. That kind of struggle helps the Type C to uncover new resources within himself, to discover that he can make it in the real world.

what about rainy days?
dad: You need to save for a rainy day.
atchity: It never rains in southern California.

Looking back on my decision to move to Los Angeles after completing my graduate work at Yale, I don't remember my father being a vital influence in my choice to take up residence in a city that rarely sees rain. But now I wonder. Being raised in his Kansas City home meant listening to the distilled wisdom by which he ruled his life, one of his favorite sayings being the necessity to save "for a rainy day."

I remember subjecting that statement to intense analysis at one point when I wanted to use nearly all my savings to buy a new car. By his definition, "a rainy day" was a day in which a sudden crisis would come along that would require an immediate infusion of cash. Like his father before him, Dad had experienced more than one such rainy day and, unlike his father, had survived because he'd prudently saved money. (My grandfather had survived by his wits.) Both had survived, each in his own way. What rainy days could possibly be in my future? I was fully insured medically and also had life insurance (both of which I've made certain to maintain throughout the career transit). My auto insurance covered accidents and injuries. Since I couldn't think of any other rainy day worth worrying about, I finally decided to set my father's proverb aside.

It's extremely important to reexamine the proverbs you inherited, and to replace them with your own. What does "A penny saved is a penny earned" mean? I thought it meant that a penny isn't worth saving because a penny will never be much more than a penny.

safety nets and catastrophe scenarios

Tightrope artists begin with a net. Before they climb to the wire, they become fully familiar with the net, testing its strength, bouncing up and down on it until they're convinced that it's safe. They face the wire and attempt new tricks only with that safety net beneath them.

I discovered that working through what I call a "catastrophe scenario" created such a safety net for me. If I couldn't make it through one of the paydays, I went from Condition Green to Condition Yellow, following Donald Trump's advice: "If you plan for the worst—if you can live with the worst—the good will always take care of itself."

In Condition Green, where the comfort horizon was a minimum of two months, I dedicated my daily schedule to long-range, high-income projects like writing new screenplays, reading books I might be able to option, or creating business plans for raising production financing. But when an unexpected event drastically shrunk the comfort horizon (a deal fell through, someone who owed money suddenly went belly up, a financier ran into financial difficulties, a distributor's check bounced), Condition Yellow kicked in.

In Condition Yellow, I have to concentrate on alternatives for the short-range and cut back on all long-range activities, except those that require a response from me rather than an initiation.

Condition Red cuts in when Condition Yellow activities seem fruitless. Because of the recession we were all blessed with in the late eighties, Condition Red occurred more than once. Condition Red requires us to focus on examining, maintaining, and mending the safety net. The safety net might include:

- Looking for a job
- Moving to a less expensive abode
- Working out a longer-term repayment plan with creditors
- Declaring bankruptcy (including knowing the telephone number for the attorney, knowing what to do first, knowing who to pay and who not to pay)
- Warning people that you are contemplating bankruptcy
- Regrouping after the battle has been lost so the war can continue

I've become so skilled at repairing the net that I've never had to use it. Something about focusing a day's activity on these fail-safe plans seems to prod fate back into your corner. Note the important omission from the Condition Red catastrophe scenario: Giving up your career is not an option. Selling popcorn at Disneyland or waiting tables is the rule rather than the exception for people in the entertainment business who haven't yet made their mark. I felt better each time I'd constructed the catastrophe scenario because I realized that, although I might suffer untold pain in the short run, nothing that happened to me in business could stop me from achieving my dream in the long run. It also helped to read about the careers of other entrepreneurs like Freddy Laker or Donald Trump. They've nearly all gone through hell before achieving their goals.

short run versus long run

The entrepreneur engaged in career transit finds himself constantly alternating between short-term needs and long-term desires. How do you determine how much energy to invest in each? How do you decide whether a detour is, instead, an entirely new route?

I try to focus on the short run only to the extent necessary to make the long run possible. Sometimes this principle makes no immediate financial sense. For instance, you need $10,000 a month to keep your chin above water. Following the Cajun proverb, "If you can touch bottom, you ain't swimmin' yet!" You're treading water month to month with $9,000 to $11,000—robbing Peter to pay Paul, juggling, tightrope walking, and so on—and your present comfort horizon is maybe two months. Note too, that seeing is believing. It isn't money that motivates the entrepreneur; it's hope. When your Mind's Eye is convinced that it sees future income, your motivation level remains high despite the Accountant's recognition that future income isn't actual income until it materializes. Accountants are conditioned to see only what's in front of their noses right now. With the unrelenting daily struggle, your Accountant's glasses sometimes need a good cleaning.

In the midst of the struggle, someone comes along and makes you "an offer you can't refuse." My own career quest hasn't been free of this temptation. It was two years after I'd produced sixteen films. My heroic path had taken a disastrous detour with the bankruptcy of Lorimar, causing my inability to retain control of

my first production company, L/A House. A financier came to me
with an offer of $15,000 monthly, indefinitely, plus shares in his
company, if I would use my marketing talents to sell orange juice
for him in Montreal, Toronto, Paris, London, Madrid, and Rome.
"What about my brilliant career in show business?" I asked. "No
problem," he replied. "You can do that on the side."

I soon found myself far from the center of filmmaking, making
what was for me an unbelievably good living selling fresh orange
juice in Europe as vice president and marketing director of a
company whose name I'd invented. For a few months I was proud
of myself because, according to what I'd read in a *USA Today*
report on American salaries, I was making more than any governor in the United States.

I learned the hard way that this is an offer you must refuse if
you want to remain true to your dreams. Although I can market
orange juice, it's not something only I can do. My dreams didn't
include marketing orange juice, and I suddenly woke up at the
Lord Byron Hotel in Rome one morning realizing how off track
I'd gotten because I was worrying about my safety on the flight
home the next day, never mind that it was first class. That was
when, as if my unconscious were intent on underscoring the reve-
lation, I lost my glasses in Antigua. Acknowledging that I wasn't
being fair to either my own career ambitions or the orange juice
czar, I resigned from the juice business.

I'm willing to call this decision to quit orange juice courageous, though I really credit it more to my learned ability to listen
to the signals from my unconscious mind than to any virtue of
consciousness. The familiar sensation of suffocation always alerts
me that all is not well.

The entrepreneur's goal is not to make money but to earn his
living doing something he loves to do. Fresh orange juice may
have been challenging, but it's not my lifetime love. When I
walked away from juicing Europe, despite the luxury of staying
at the best hotels in those wonderfully romantic capitals, I knew
in my gut I was doing the right thing. My faithful assistant, Jane

Singer, who'd suffered through the detour with me, congratulated me on the decision, even though we both knew it probably meant the end of our working relationship. "This is the best decision you've made in a long time," she told me. I'd gotten back on track by renouncing the temptation of money. I don't need to tell you how my father reacted to this news.

The detour reconfirms the route. Although I falter now and then, I've learned to no longer question the shape of the career I've chosen to pursue. I've gotten my act together. All other considerations are secondary to that, though I've learned that, for the Type C, being yourself is first and foremost a process. Knowing yourself is the most challenging education of all, the final frontier. And nothing teaches you more about yourself than making a career transition in a world in love with pigeonholes and niches.

money and self-esteem

porgy: I got plenty of nothing, and nothing's plenty for me.
atchity: If the choice is wealth or dreams, I choose dreams.

Too many people associate their self-esteem with how much money they have, either in their pockets, in the bank, in assets, or in receivables. Career transition has taught me to count the money in my pocket rather than the money in the bank or the future as sufficient for my present mood. As always, my unconscious was way ahead of me on this. I vividly remember the day I realized that every time I took money from the ATM I automatically began humming the song about "a pocket full of beans, a new pair of jeans." The physical act of putting money in my pocket gave me enough confidence for the day.

It's easy to talk positively when you're feeling optimistic, but when the prospects of getting through payday without going to Condition Red are dim, you're rarely feeling optimistic. That's okay. Go away, as they say, "for the whistle." Take whatever time you need to work through your dark feelings because you must work through them one way or another before your head will be clear enough to figure out new solutions to the present crisis. By watching my behavior over the years, I discovered that the worst of times are the weekends that fall before a first or fifteenth during a Condition Yellow. I used to spend these weekends in intense anxiety because there was little I could do over the weekend to solve the problem I imagined would plop itself squarely in my face by Monday morning.

After years of this behavior, burning out a number of wonderful Zuma Beach and Central Park moments along the way, my Mind's Eye realized a couple of things:

- The Monday Morning Problem was never as urgent as I had imagined it would be
- Whatever happened on Monday morning happened regardless of how I felt over the weekend

Every time I went through the down-cycle depression of these weekends, I emerged with solutions that allowed me to deal with the Monday Morning Problem.

From these observations, my Mind's Eye concluded that my life would be more pleasant if I decided on Friday that I would limit the anxiety to part of the weekend instead of all of it, and spend that anxious part either alone or with a friend who would provide perspective. I've even managed to see my way through some Condition Yellow weekends with no anxiety, by making myself list the solutions on Friday rather than waiting to struggle through the soul-searching that would inevitably lead to writing them down Sunday evening.

It's okay to give anxiety license, as long as you've managed it by compartmentalizing in this fashion. Once you give it license, the anxiety isn't nearly as interested in laying you low as it was when you allowed yourself to be tortured by it.

Part of the intensity of these weekend anxieties was rooted in how I felt about myself when things looked bad financially for Monday morning. I had to work through feeling like a failure, work against the image of my father worrying, so many years ago, about how I was going to earn a living. My self-esteem was still tied up with money, no matter how few beans had to be in my pocket to get that song going. I'm not sure you can ever completely overcome this ingrained hardwiring. But having your Mind's Eye become aware of it is a tremendous step toward managing it on a daily basis.

the wolf at the door

well meaning friend: How are things going?
atchity: *Where* things are going is all that really matters.

One of the reasons I prefer business to being an academic (as in a cocktail party exchange I overheard recently: "Are you academic, too?" a professor asked the woman I was with. "No," she replied. "I take iron.") is that businesspeople aren't afraid to use clichés that portray life more vividly than precisely invented original language.

"How are things going?" I once asked a fellow entrepreneur.

"We're about to go belly up," he replied, shaking his head.

I could tell by the way he carried himself that "going belly up" wasn't necessarily the end of the world. The metaphor gave him detachment. Using the language of the game brings perspective. As long as you realize it's a game, you're still in charge. If you don't, the clichés can kill you. You've got to learn to master them.

"What would you do," a student in a weekend career transit workshop in Minneapolis asked me, "if you ended up face down on the pavement in a pool of blood?"

"How deep is the blood?" I wanted to know. If it's not too deep and I haven't drowned in it, and I can't walk because "they" broke my legs, then the answer is, "Crawl forward."

The cliché that used to concern me the most, as I explained to Dr. Joyce Brothers, was the wolf at the door. I finally learned that dealing with the wolf at the door begins with walking to the door, having your Mind's Eye do a reality check, then talking to your Accountant about its choice of vocabulary. If there is no actual wolf at the actual door, you're okay. The wolf is a product of the Type C imagination (terrified Visionary and naysaying Accountant conspiring to frighten you), and your imagination can be tamed by your Mind's Eye.

Examine the financial metaphors that the clichés of family, friends, and associates inflict upon you, then make them your own.

they: He doesn't have a pot to piss in.
mind's eye: Thank God that's true. I have a state-of-the-art flush toilet that's infinitely preferable.
they: He spends money like it's going out of style.
mind's eye: But that isn't likely to happen soon, so there's no problem.
they: You're robbing Peter to pay Paul.
mind's eye: Exactly. Then I rob Paul to pay Peter. It all balances out.
they: What will you do when that rainy day comes?
mind's eye: Rejoice. We always need rain in southern California.

As Humpty Dumpty told Alice, "Words mean what I want them to mean." It's a question of who is the master—them or us.

I used to imagine returning to Los Angeles from a business trip where all hadn't worked out as well as I'd hoped, that "the guys" would meet my plane at Los Angeles International and lead me away in handcuffs ("the guys" being suits from American Express, MasterCard, VISA, and Discover). It hasn't happened yet, and that's simply not how it works in our country, but the metaphor still entertains my debarkations from time to time.

burning bridges and striking tents

Type C career transit candidates want to know: "When do I burn my bridges?" Burning bridges means cutting yourself off from your former career so that you're forced to devote all your

energies to your new career. While I was in production with the
first eight Lorimar films, I burned my bridges by resigning from
Occidental College. Before that moment I'd been shuttling back
and forth across the career bridge like Stonewall Jackson's Army of
Virginia—fighting the battles on both sides—by taking first one,
then another, yearlong leave of absence. But the decision to take
a leave of absence without pay came as a result of very specific
symptoms. I'd reached the point in my new career where the
development of my film projects was becoming intense; I was
wanted on the phone constantly. Meanwhile, I'd be sitting in my
office at the college conferring with students about their con-
cerns. The phone would ring, interrupting the conference. When
this began to happen regularly, I realized that my two careers had
reached the conflict point. I wasn't being fair to either by trying
to shuttle back and forth on the bridge.

Only you can define your conflict point, and sometimes it can't
be defined in advance. You'll simply recognize it when it arrives.
In general, you burn your bridges when you're forced to choose
between one shore and the other. And, of course, the courageous
Type C will choose in favor of the new, Type C, career.

But don't burn your bridges before you feel you either have to,
or can afford to. I burned mine only when I'd attained a comfort
horizon of two years. One of my clients announced to me six
months into his first novel that he was thinking of taking early
retirement in order to devote all his time to his writing. His family
wasn't thrilled with the prospect, but after grilling him about his
retirement income, I encouraged him to move forward. He was
using the opportunity to test my belief in him, and I had no
doubts about his talent. He's now retired, having finished out his
last year of "work," and happily halfway through his third novel.

redefining financial security

My client got to this point by redefining his needs for financial
security. If he was now making $4,000 a month, and living com-
fortably but unhappily, because he had so little time to write, how

would he feel making $3,000 monthly, living more cautiously but having an additional minimum of eight hours a day to write? Even his family came around when he helped them visualize the change in his temperament.

The self-esteem that begins to creep in when you've firmly decided to go for it will bring you the strength to deal forthrightly and creatively with bills, creditors, and all the issues surrounding money in general.

invest in yourself!

It never ceases to amaze me when people who claim to be making a career transit hesitate about investing money to expedite that transit. One side of them has their priorities straight, the other is trying to sabotage them. One of my workshop students recently asked me if she could pay the workshop fee in installments. She started to rattle off all the expenses she had with her business and family. When I interrupted her, "Of course you can partially defer the fee, if you really need to. Do you really need to? Think about it and what kind of statement you're making to yourself." She continued with her list, then paused. "I'll call you back," she said.

When she did call back, she was elated. She'd had a long discussion with her husband, who told her she should be investing in her new career. "So I want to pay the whole fee up front," she added. My question had made her stop to think and get her head together. She recognized that the Accountant was using lists of expenses as a means of telling her she wasn't worthy of the luxury of a career transition.

In situations like this, people also somehow lose their business common sense, which tells them that any new business requires an investment of money as well as thought, time, and energy; and that it will profit from the experience of experts. People who resist the investment are indulging in magical thinking, and would rather risk wasting years on wild goose chases than availing themselves of professional shortcuts. The money you spend on books, workshops, and consultants—if you've selected them carefully through common-sense questions and reference checking—may save you ten times as much as you'd spend learning on your own. By definition, second careers are more time-sensitive than first ones, where, in the expansiveness of youth, we think nothing of making the same mistake over and over again.

Anything or anyone who can help you move more quickly toward your dream career is a smart investment. Refusing to make such investments may be your Accountant's way of sabotaging this very threatening Type C career transit. The money you spend is only money. The time you waste is the only time you have.

creative money management

When things are going well financially and there's plenty of money, of course you'll pay everything on time—even ahead of time—to rest assured that your comfort horizon has been secured. But when things get rough, here are some hints for dealing with your career transit finances, gleaned from my experiences along the way.

REDUCE YOUR OVERHEAD

Every dollar that goes to overhead reduces the longevity of your career transit. Toughing it out in the short-run ensures your long-run success. Besides, toughing it out is more romantic: candlelight at home instead of at a posh restaurant; eating lobster at home instead of out; renting two DVDs and turning off the phone instead of spending money on an evening at the cinema.

YOU DON'T HAVE TO PAY ALL YOUR BILLS ON TIME

Ideally, you might say, it would be great to pay early (you receive a large check and pay your rent three months in advance). If that's an expression of your Type C creativity, do it. Otherwise, realize that not even your Accountant wants you to pay early. When I can, I pay early just to remind myself who's the master. If you're late, of course, you pay penalties—but so what? I've overheard people talking about how much they hate to pay late charges. "How much was the late charge?" I asked. "Sixteen dollars!" they replied, "but it's the principle of the thing." Well, if you're working a secure job, focused on security as a primary value, then that very well may be an important principle to you. For the Type C personality, the principle of the thing is paying when you can pay. You don't mind being penalized when you can't pay because penalties are part of the game. How good a hockey player would you be if you were so worried about the penalty box that you never got close to the opposing players? Pay when you can, and don't worry about it. Does this sound dangerous to you? You're probably not a Type C.

YOU DON'T HAVE TO PAY EVERYTHING THAT'S DUE EACH TIME

Pay something. Pay what you can. In the long run, only total non-payment destroys your credit. Imperfect credit is so normal it's not worth worrying about if you've already chosen the path of the Type C.

YOUR CREDIT RATING IS IMPORTANT, NOT ALL-IMPORTANT!

But your dream is. And the dream, once it arrives, will over-shadow the credit rating. Credit ratings aren't cast in stone, either. If you have the skills to succeed at the level of your dreams, you'll have the skills to get what you want, with or without a perfect credit rating.

IMPROVISE

There are many ways to keep the computers out there happy. Happy computers are busy computers. One entrepreneur told me that when his receivables didn't arrive in time to make his payments, he'd put pinholes in all his checks so that the computers would kick them back. Then he replaced them, one by one, as the receivables trickled in. I'm not recommending this method, but I am recommending that you apply your Type C creativity to the

Accountants' world that keeps bringing those paydays around with such relentless regularity.

JUGGLE MONEY EVERY TWO WEEKS, NOT EVERY DAY

You can worry about your financial problems daily, even hourly, but that's giving money an awful lot of control over your life. You acquire a clear-cut illusion of control if you postpone major worry sessions to the first and fifteenth of the month—or maybe the day before each.

WRITE YOUR CHECKS ON TIME, SEND THEM OUT ON *YOUR* TIME

It gives me the illusion of control to know that the checks are waiting to go out as soon as the universe cooperates and provides sufficient balance to send them. Even when I have money, I send only one check out at a time—choosing to control the outflow.

ROB PETER TO PAY PAUL

Having several accounts helps. Of course, you may run out of juggling room at some point, but that's what Condition Yellow is all about.

MAKE THEM BEG A LITTLE

Dad, I know this sounds terrible, but why should I be in such a hurry to pay every bill exactly when it's due? Obviously, you should do so when you have plenty of money available, and you do so when the debt is owed to an individual whose personal finances are affected by it.

But during those dry spells, when you don't have plenty of cash available, hold off paying the others as long as you can. I've known affluent people who pay their bills only when the pressure becomes extreme. At first, I found this behavior hard to reconcile with their possession of such hefty bank accounts. Now I wonder if it explains why they remain wealthy. They aren't in a hurry to pay up. At the very least, don't be in such a hurry.

THE CHECK IS IN THE MAIL

How many times have people told you that? Why aren't you using the same tool once in a while?

TAKING ADVANTAGE OF THE OBVIOUS

MasterCard and VISA have funded a goodly number of career changes. Once my dry cleaner, who'd arrived in Beverly Hills from Iran less than a year before, looked worried when he made his weekly drop-off. I asked him why. He told me he'd opened up a second shop.

"Already?" I said. "Business must be great."

"It could be better. I used MasterCard," he told me. He'd been issued a credit line and used it to the max. A year later, he'd opened up his third shop. That's the spirit! After surviving life under the Shah and the Ayatollah he figured, "What's the worst that can happen to me in America?"

USE YOUR OWN CREATIVITY TO TAKE CONTROL OF MONEY

Most Type Cs have, at best, an ambivalent relationship with money. I remember once telling a therapist that I felt bad about crumpling my bills into a wad in my pocket, instead of folding them neatly into my money clip. I felt my father would disapprove.

"How much money would you estimate you've lost in your lifetime because you wad your bills up?" she asked.

I gave it some thought. "A few dollars maybe," I said.

She'd made her point. Wadded money was just as good as folded money, but with one significant difference. It sometimes makes the Type C feel better to crumple it. Money is the means to an end, not the end in itself.

For a long time I made a practice of depositing in a savings account all the checks I received with odd cents in the total ($5.61, $281.43, etc.). I didn't like all the rules I'd grown up with about how to save money, so I invented one that I could call my own. Once, when Roy Disney told his brother Walt that the bank was adamant they catch up on a $20 million loan, on which several installments had been missed, Walt replied that he'd solve the problem by asking them for an additional $20 million. Roy hit the ceiling, demanding to know how Walt could even think they'd agree under the circumstances. Walt was puzzled by Roy's response. "What choice do they have?" Walt asked him.

GAMBLE ONLY ON YOUR SELF-INVESTMENT

Play the lottery from time to time, but don't invest more than a few minutes gambling at the slots, crap table, or stock market. Early in my career transit, my then wife discovered a stock she wanted us to invest in. I agreed to contribute part of the investment; then I changed my mind. The more I thought about it, the less sense it made. I knew my career change would involve all my powers and resources, and more money than I could foresee. I explained to her that I didn't feel right about investing in anything other than what I was going for. Stock market investment is a crapshoot over which the investor has zero control. I have a good deal of control over the pursuit of my dream. Your best asset is yourself. As long as funds are limited, you are your best investment.

EXPECT TO INVEST MONEY IN YOUR CAREER, AS WELL AS TIME AND ENERGY

Businesspeople expect new investments to cost money. Take a businesslike approach, but evaluate each expenditure cautiously, doing your best to make sure that the money is being well spent.

USE THE RESOURCES AROUND YOU

When the wolves are howling around the answering machine and you've done all you can to fend them off on your own, consult one of the many services available to help you manage your creditors. That's where the Accountants shine. Don't forget to use them. You'll learn much about the resiliency built into the American system.

DON'T BE AFRAID OF THE IRS

Keep records. As an entrepreneur, you're more likely to be audited than you were as an inhabitant of a secure day job. It's not because they hate Type C personalities, it's because they understand the pressures entrepreneurs are under and want to make sure the pressures don't lead to tax evasion. My father taught me to type tax returns for his clients when I was six. Ever since, I'd regarded the IRS as the fiercest dragon in my hero's journey. But after coming through a three-year audit with flying colors, I'm delighted to report that my onboard Accountant's insistence on record keeping tamed the dragon. Yes, they did ask for records. Yes, I spent a number of miserable hours preparing them. Yes, they asked for explanations and an account of my business activities. But, working through my CPA, I satisfied them. I had taken business deductions aggressively, and in the end all my deductions were accepted. In fact, after he'd finished, the inspector told my CPA that everyone should take deductions as aggressively.

Throughout the process I felt my self-confidence increasing. What had begun as fear of the unknown was becoming a familiar battle, in which my role was to bring in the ammunition and weapons from my arsenal and continue bombarding the enemy with my resources. I'm good at that. And the battle was won.

WHEN I HAVE MONEY, EVERYBODY HAS MONEY

Rick McKeown, my entrepreneur brother-in-law, is the first one I heard in my adult life stating what I now know is the universal catechism of all those who don't have a regular cash flow. But growing up, the statement came out as a negative from my father, like this: "With him, it's either feast or famine." It's taken me all my life to realize I don't mind the feast-or-famine scenario. I happen to love feasts and, as a former old-fashioned Catholic, can appreciate fasting. If the alternative is a sensible three meals a day, every day, I'm with Rick. Don't let the metaphors grind you down.

SERIOUSLY, HOW BAD WOULD IT BE TO GET A JOB OR KEEP YOUR PRESENT JOB?

An actress explained to me that she'd managed to earn a good living for the first three years of her new career, but that this year had been tough and she was about to go back to waitressing (which she'd done before her first gig). "That's great," I congratulated her.

She looked surprised, then realized that I understood. I thought it was great that she could so easily slip back into a day job as undemanding of psychological resources, as flexible with schedules, and as easy to leave behind the moment a major role came her way. Don't let your pride stand in the way of taking care of business and doing what has to be done. Your pride should be invested entirely in the ultimate fulfillment of your dream, and what must be done along the way is only a means to that end.

"WHEN PROSPERITY COMES, DO NOT USE ALL OF IT"

I believe it was Confucius who stated this maxim, and it's worth heeding. Once your Type C dream begins to generate income, you'll experience the sweet sensation of being compensated for being yourself. If you're good at it, the compensation may suddenly increase dramatically. You may strike it rich! If that happens, don't forget that your highest value is the freedom to continue pursuing your dreams. Buy more of that freedom by holding onto some of the abundance you've earned. You see how my father's rainy-day philosophy has evolved.

8

your mind/body asset base

motto of jesuit order: *Mens sana, in corpore sano.* (A sound mind, in a sound body.)
atchity: Surely you jest.
arab saying: On the day of victory, no one is tired.
atchity: Until then, no one dies of exhaustion.

Once you get through the madness of making a career transit and have constructed an operating plan, all focus must be on methods for implementation. Only method counters exhaustion. Rebuilding your own Type C, positive reinforcement on a daily, sometimes hourly, basis requires an operating plan that's firmly tied to your dream—and consistent discipline to move forward despite all obstacles or considerations.

At the same time you must become more adept at avoiding negative reinforcement of all kinds: symbolic, personal, psychological, family, and physical. You must also short-circuit the need for immediate reinforcement if you wish to accomplish something grander than anything you've previously accomplished. As much as I enjoyed writing them, I stopped doing regular book reviews for the *Los Angeles Times* when I committed to my career change. The reviews gave me immediate rewards but drained energy and time from the long-range dream.

physical health

press: Why did we invade Grenada, Mr. President?
reagan: Because nutmeg comes from Grenada. No Grenada, no
nutmeg. No nutmeg—no Christmas!
atchity: No health, no energy—no dream.

During my first career, my efforts to maintain a sound body were
sporadic, at best. But the career transit has forced me into health.
I can't afford sick days because *I am* the business, and without my
healthy activity level, things don't move forward rapidly enough to
satisfy me. In the last five years I've exchanged aspirin, blood pressure medication, antibiotics, and prescription sleeping pills for
Chinese herbs that maintain all the foibles of my system without
the unpleasant side effects. I use the treadmill at least three times
weekly, and try to play tennis or walk the other four days. Fighting
with my weight had been a constant struggle, but I made progress
and lost the twenty pounds I needed to lose by finally embracing
the Atkins way of eating as my regular routine—or if I'm eating
something I shouldn't, only eating half of it. I try to get a regular
massage once a week, and a deep-tissue massage at least every other
week. I pursue every lead I hear about that promises greater health,
because I need all the energy I can get to achieve my dreams.

I used to feel a little odd about what others might call fanati-
cism, even though I live in Los Angeles, the health fanatic capital
of the planet. (Angelenos cheerfully admit there may be healthier
beings in other galaxies.) But then one of my clients invited me
to join him at a nearby health spa for an evening of sauna, steam
room, and hot and cold springs. On the way I asked him how
often he visited the spa. He said he tried to make it once a week,
but at least every other week.

"You do more body stuff, and more head stuff, than anyone
I know," I remarked. He had just turned me on to blue-green
algae, as well as to an herbalist.

"That's right. I do everything I can think of. Gotta take care of
my chief asset."

Which is exactly the point. Luxuriate in taking care of yourself. Now that you've gone for it, and are committed to following your dream, you owe it to yourself to take care of your Type C body. Regard all health-improvement expenditures as priorities, and don't defer them until "you make it big." One hour of exercise in the morning is probably worth two extra hours of sleep. One of our producer friends, Warren Zide (*American Pie, Final Destination*), has gotten up at 5:00 A.M. to spend two hours at the gym before work ever since he was an assistant agent at ICM.

I rarely lose a night's sleep, despite the stressful lifestyle I've chosen, because I promised myself at the start of my career transit that losing sleep over this new career was a symptom of not being able to handle it. Take your sleep very seriously. The minimum you require for functioning with a clear and rested brain is a nonnegotiable need. But make sure you've done everything you can to make your sleep restful. To begin with, unless you're allergic to cotton, buy an all-cotton mattress with an all-cotton cover that breathes through the night instead of emitting noxious fumes. Engage only in soothing activities before falling asleep (sex is best during the day). And if you have a telephone in the bedroom or anywhere near (I no longer do), disconnect it! If you know you might be disturbed, you're already disturbed. I don't watch television news before falling asleep because it fills my head with incoming stimuli at a time when I need to shut down the onboard computer so it can reshuffle and sort its programs. Instead, I find reading a half-page of almost anything will instantly knock me out, no matter how charged-up I felt before I began reading.

If you're going all out in your rush toward that metaphorical wallgate, you'll still get tired. But you'll know enough about yourself to recognize the difference between physical or psychological fatigue and depression. My herbalist told me that, since I use my brain so much, I needed to take herbs to cool it and calm it down. I thought he was nuts, but I tried it. Metagenics TCB3 (a combination of various herbs) does, in fact, calm your brain down. I rarely get headaches, and almost always sleep soundly (full moons are the exception).

Even on the day before victory, fatigue may be a constant companion dogging your heels. Don't confuse your exhaustion with anything other than its physical reality. Fatigue is neither a psychological warning that you've moved to the far side of madness, nor a sign that you've overreached your limits. It is especially not a mystical command to go to work for the post office. Guard against fatigue through foreknowledge of your own system, when you care to apply it, and through regular physical exercise and frequent vacations.

emotions, mood, and attitude

FDR: The only thing we have to fear is fear itself.
atchity: No wonder we have our hands full.

The key to an entrepreneur's success in life is his present mood. "The way things are going," as Robert L. Kuhn noted, "is more important than the way things are."

I've found it useful, at various turning points in my career transit, to keep track of my mood on a scale of 0 to 5 (5 being the best)—jotting today's rating on my day-runner page or in my journal. Somehow the simple act of recording it betters the mood.

5—**Complete optimism**. Things couldn't be going better. I'm looking at the Promised Land.

4—**Things are going great**. I can see the light at the end of the tunnel.

3—**What happened**? We're in a stall.

2—**I've faced worse than this**.

1—**How are we going to get out of this one**? Time to mend the safety net.

0—**Condition Red**. Total disaster. Time for the farm.

Usually, after a few days of recording your mood rating, you'll find that you no longer need this little trick because the mood-rating scale brings internal perspective. Compare today's crisis to ones you've weathered before, and remind yourself that you've already faced this challenge and dealt with it successfully, that you've faced more complex crises than today's, and that, with any luck, you'll someday face more complex ones than you can even imagine now. Remind yourself that your mood has been lower. Finally, when your mood sinks to 0 or hovers near 1, remind yourself that you're about to turn a corner because it's always darkest before the dawn.

My phone mania was interrupted one particularly stressful day by the ringing of the doorbell. It was the plumber, coming to fix the toilet. I directed him toward the bathroom and went back to the unruly phones. In the middle of my next conference call, I realized that I was having difficulty hearing because of the noise coming from the bathroom. I hung up, becoming less annoyed and more interested as I headed down the hall toward its source. The plumber was on his knees, working on the toilet, singing at the top of his lungs.

"Are you always this cheerful?" I finally asked.

"You bet I am," he said.

"Why?"

"Because that's my attitude. All I got is my attitude."

"Your attitude?"

"They can take my job away. I can go home and find they've taken my old lady away. They can even take my home away, but they can't take away my attitude!"

The psychologist Viktor E. Frankl must have encountered the same plumber. Frankl says that the last great human freedom is the freedom to determine your own attitude. Once attitude is determined for the positive, the next step is protecting it and thereby protecting the energy that positive attitude brings to daily life.

perspective and self-investment

karl menninger: Attitudes are more important than facts.

atchity: Minute by minute, my attitude is my greatest achievement.

The Visionary is generally so intense and concentrated that he loses sight of the forest for the trees. The present crisis is the end of the world. Today's problems are the worst ever. Perspective is therefore the most crucial helpmate your Mind's Eye can provide. Perspective comes in two varieties: perspective toward yourself, and perspective toward others.

When people all over the world are dying in ethnic conflagrations and from starvation, how upset am I allowed to be over a financier not returning my call for two days? External perspective derives from the ancient observation that there isn't a shred of evidence in human history suggesting that life should be taken seriously. Of course, the Accountant takes life seriously, which is why he's often anxious; but that's why he needs to be finessed. But the Visionary takes his Vision with equal seriousness, which is why he's often terrified. Your Mind's Eye takes your work, not yourself, seriously. Donald Trump, in *The Art of the Deal*, puts it this way:

> One of the keys to thinking big is total focus. I think of it almost as a controlled neurosis, which is a quality I've noticed in many highly successful entrepreneurs. They're obsessive, they're driven, they're single-minded and sometimes they're almost maniacal, but it's all channeled into their work.

Taking your vision seriously must be clearly distinguished from the futile rigors of self-involvement. Self-involvement is narcissism in isolation, leading nowhere, with nothing to offer outside yourself. Self-investment is self-involvement turned toward action in the public arena. When you're self-invested, you do the best you can and leave the rest up to the Fate that watches over the efforts of entrepreneurs.

high anxiety: "can't live with it, can't dream without it"

Every entrepreneur I know wishes he could reduce the anxiety level of career transit. Yet most would also agree that without anxiety creativity would die. Anxiety is just the Accountant's word for what the Mind's Eye redefines as the excitement of the chase. Fear threatens the entrepreneur's every move. When you're concentrating on walking across the razor's edge, your imagination magnifies every sensation you encounter. Frank Herbert, in *Dune*, offers this incantation to ward off fear:

> I must not fear. Fear is the mind-killer. Fear is the little death that brings instant obliteration. I will face my fear. I will permit it to pass over me and through me. And when it has gone past I will turn the inner eye to see its path. Where the fear has gone there will be nothing. Only I will remain.

The trick is to allow your Mind's Eye to take control of the anxiety, claiming it as your own territory, redefining it as something closer to the heart's desire without losing its effectiveness as a goad to action. Working your caduceus through vocabulary transformations—*anxiety* becomes *uncertainty* becomes *elation*. Excitation is a sign of life—a good sign. Never forget that this particular rush of energy you've called "anxiety" is your own characteristic creation, the threshold of your dream. Honor it by renaming it in your own best image.

talking to yourself

cajun proverb: If you not talking to yourself first, you talking to the wrong person.
atchity: Just make sure you're listening.

Others have confirmed the usefulness of talking to yourself (see, for example, Shad Helmstetter's *What to Say When You Talk to Yourself*). Talking to the Accountant and the Visionary during a moment of crisis can be enormously illuminating, though sometimes your Mind's Eye has to trick you into the conversation by jumping into the middle of one of those familiar internal debates that always seem to come out the same way.

Here's a typical example: You're sitting alone at a restaurant on a business trip. You aren't really that hungry, but you're telling yourself you deserve to eat something nice because you've had a hard trip. Your eyes scan the selections, one part of your brain pushing for the salad, the other pushing for the prime rib. Wait a minute, you say to yourself. How can I be thinking of the prime rib when I know it's not good for me and would be a waste of money because I'm not even that hungry? But, the other part is saying, you deserve the prime rib. This is a great restaurant. Why eat only salad? Celebrate. You are about to enter what I call the Zone, that period of lost control that takes over the moment the waiter arrives and you change, "I'll have the tossed salad" to "I'll have the prime rib," as though a demon had taken control of your tongue.

To break through the Zone, your Mind's Eye has to jump into the conversation:

"Who said celebrate?"

With your Mind's Eye, you round up the usual suspects: the Accountant and the Visionary. The Accountant, because he's measuring what you deserve or don't deserve, and the price of things; the Visionary, because he's so excited by the prime rib and feels like celebrating.

Consider this scenario: You plan in advance not to gorge yourself at a meal. You have every intention of sticking to your plan, but the last moment you pig out. Then you suffer immediate remorse. What's really happening here is a Visionary override that takes you into that Zone. Your Mind's Eye and your Accountant know what should be done, but the Visionary, in its extreme neediness and complete lack of foresight, simply overrides all the sensibleness and takes over to create its Zone of Control. Afterwards, the others click in again—too late. The Accountant grumbling that you just gained five pounds and wasted money, your Mind's Eye wondering how it lost control of the situation.

Becoming aware of who's talking is the only way to break out of this pattern and escape from the Zone. The Accountant is saying the roast beef would be a waste of money because you're not even that hungry. But the Visionary insists, "I deserve the prime rib. This is a great restaurant. Why eat only salad? Let's celebrate." If awareness prevails, the Mind's Eye may finally placate both the Accountant and the Visionary by ordering a celebratory shrimp cocktail and the salad, or maybe even a festive Caesar salad. If the Visionary is particularly adamant, the Mind's Eye may even order the prime rib, with the stipulation that you'll eat only a few bites then ask that your plate be removed. And you feel better about yourself when you get back to your room.

It comes down to which voice you'll recognize as the best you.

The hedonistic Visionary lives to eat; the Puritanical Accountant eats to live. Neither satisfies the Type C, whose Mind's Eye is determined to find the exact balance that allows us to eat well in a celebratory manner at each meal. The Mind's Eye's discovery proceeds by jumping into the middle of these debates and interrupting the pattern. Make the next restaurant menu you encounter a test of your ability to identify the various voices, awaken your Mind's Eye to manage them to your benefit, and escape the self-destructive Zone. Pick and choose. Don't be afraid to ask for half portions, or to leave half your meal on the plate. Once you've left your parents' house, "Eat everything on your plate" is no longer an appropriate admonition. And money is certainly not the issue. If you can afford to eat in restaurants at all, you can afford to take liberties with the menu. In the long run it even makes economic sense for you to order several expensive but relatively healthy dishes and pick and choose what you like from them. Eat what's good for you, and what's fun, in a combination that makes long-range sense. Don't worry about being considered eccentric by your companions, by the waiter, or by the management. You *are* eccentric. You're a Type C.

energy management

Managing your energy is one of the most vital steps in the self-knowing process that leads to satisfaction in the creative life. The process begins by allowing your Mind's Eye to take an inventory of how you feel day in and day out. Most people know something about themselves in this regard: "I'm a night owl," or "I'm a morning person." But it's also important to know which activities drain you and which invigorate you. I schedule lectures and seminars as interruptions to a long siege of writing because standing up teaching all day invigorates me as much as it might drain someone else. Going to meetings, on the other hand, saps my energy. I need to play tennis afterwards, or take a cold shower, or hit the treadmill to regain my energy.

Energy isn't constant. It operates on an ebb and flow principle that varies from person to person. When you're experiencing a surge of energy, it's time to reach out—make sales calls, follow up, close deals, tackle a particularly thorny challenge. When your energy is ebbing, it's time to withdraw into an activity that restores your energy—reading and writing in solitude, taking a quick nap, going for a walk, whatever invigorates you.

Because your dream's success often depends on the image you present to the public—and because you recognize the enormous energy it requires to keep this image shining when, deep down, you're exhausted from the effort—you'll learn to keep a high public profile when you're up and to maintain a lower profile when you're down. After all, you are selling the confidence in your voice and in your posture. Don't risk the sales call when the energy's not there.

instincts

Before my career transit, I used to say, "I'd love to follow my instincts, if I could just find the damned things." Throwing yourself into a new career restores your instincts. Because I knew nothing about what I was going to be every day, I was forced to listen for my inner voices, forced to recognize and discover my own Mind's Eye. The biggest mistakes I've made in the past ten years resulted from not following my initial instincts, including what I call the "Life Is Too Short Response."

In order to discover your Mind's Eye, you'll have to fight the Accountant, who is fighting for the control he's used to exerting over your practical daily routine. And he'll win some, if not most, of the time at first. You can get around him by keeping track of his responses and comparing them to the outcome of following your Mind's Eye's instincts instead.

Here's a typical example: A woman dressed entirely in orange approaches you with her plan to introduce a new toy into the market. She has a booklet and a video clip prepared that you immediately recognize as something that should never be shown to a publisher or production company. They aren't professional, and are tattered around the edges. They are orange. She has a homemade mockup that she says was done by a company in New York. Her makeup is askew and, though the day is cool, she looks like she's just driven through a forest fire. After telling you her entire medical history from birth on, she explains that she wants you to take over the project, help her make the sale, help produce the book, the film, the TV series, the videos, the toys.

Even though you're not in the toy business, your Visionary sees, beneath the surface, that the idea is cute. Your Accountant adds that less cute ideas have made fortunes. Before you know it, you're talking about what you can do to help—your connections with children's book editors, your relationships with animation houses, and so on. Meanwhile, your Mind's Eye is tugging at your sleeves, saying, "Life's too short."

You ignore the tugging, and six months later totally regret it. The project is a waste of time because its creator is her own worst enemy, impossible to deal with, unwilling to be pinned down to a deal, paranoid, suspicious—and probably downplaying her medical record. You ease your way out of the situation, swearing to yourself that you'll listen to your instincts next time. Your Mind's Eye's gentle tugging at the sleeve was more important than the Visionary's shout or the Accountant's quiet abacus.

The next time a woman in orange arrives, your Mind's Eye has a better chance of winning the argument.

If you could find the circuit box that controls self-defeating and self-sabotaging behavior, like pursuing a sidetrack despite the "Life Is Too Short Response," it would be relatively easy to open it up and check the circuits.

The circuit box is your mind, and, with enough awareness and persistence, you can open it up.

mind

wallace stevens: It is never satisfied, the mind. Never.

type C: Maybe that's why I try to take vacations from my mind whenever possible.

Mood becomes attitude becomes language becomes action becomes reaction-and-results becomes a dream fulfilled. But for those educated in the traditions of Western civilization, seasoned in reason and logic, all too often dream manifests first in thought. For us the progression reads, *dream* becomes *thought* becomes *mood* becomes *attitude*.

We all know that the mind plays tricks on us, one of the most familiar being selective memory capacity. While we're sleeping or simply growing older, our mind is busy revising scenes from the past to fit our present needs. Jung called it "selective perception;" that uncanny ability of the mind to see owls everywhere—on coins, coats of arms, belt buckles, and bath towels—once you've decided to write a book about owls. Psychologists call a victim's sharp recollection of the gun used to fire at them "weapon focus," as in: "I don't remember his face, but it was a .38 caliber, black-barreled gun, with a rosewood handle." One of the worst mind slips I've come across is an actor friend who told me the story of his second divorce. "Two years into our marriage," he said, "we were having a party and I turned to introduce a guest to my wife—and couldn't remember her name. Jeremy, this is my wife—what's-her-name."

Pay more attention to what happens than to what you think is happening, just as you should pay more attention to what people do than to what they say. When your mind, without your cooperation, causes traffic accidents; loses billfolds, wristwatches, eyeglasses; or forgets your wife's name, your Mind's Eye has not yet been awakened and put in charge. Minds performing tricks like these are desperately signaling that the inner conflict must come to an end. The animals in the ring are running amok because the ringmaster is out to lunch.

magical thinking

One of the most common tricks of the untamed mind—one that damages the Type C's career transit—is magical thinking, an extraordinary sabotage mechanism arising primarily from the Visionary, which undermines progress toward the dream. Uncontrolled magical thinking slows the Type C's forward mom-entum, and creates a negative attitude of victimization. A typical example of magical thinking is neglecting to follow up on a solicitation, hoping that your prospect is taking a long time to answer because "It must be under serious consideration." Months go by and you finally call to follow up, only to discover that they didn't receive what you sent. Destructive magical thinking takes the adage "no news is good news" seriously. Magical thinking is finding an agent to handle your sales for you because "I'm just not good at selling," then discovering that you're spending as much time bugging the agent as you would be bugging the potential customers—and much less productively.

The Accountant cooperates in magical thinking because the Accountant hates rejection. The longer the Accountant postpones a phone call, the longer he puts off what he fears may be a negative response.

When the Mind's Eye takes over:

- We keep our sharpest, "third" eye on the ball.
- We automatically follow up every solicitation with a phone call "just to make sure you received my letter."

- We automatically construct a linkage to the next step:
  "When should I call you for a response?"
- We calendar the two weeks the prospect asked for and,
  allowing another day or so for courtesy, call back and say,
  "You asked me to call in two weeks."

Uncontrolled magical thinking has been replaced with reality-based, productive, confidence-inspiring behavior.

The Mind's Eye, as the most sophisticated of the Type C's three minds, recognizes that magical thinking may indeed play a constructive role in relation to mood and self-confidence. When you breakfast on hope every day, you must do your shopping somewhere. The more experienced you become, the more you know where to find hope at the best prices—even inventing it, if need be, by allowing some illusions to continue until a more satisfying nut falls into your bowl. Then you can discard the other, like a man who discards a shaky wooden crutch for a reinforced aluminum one. He would be foolish to discard the wooden crutch before he got his hands on the replacement. Your Mind's Eye allows magical thinking when hope is in need of buttressing, but only to get through that low moment.

Here's an example: It's Friday afternoon. You've had a rough week of defeated expectations, and you know you'll spend the weekend struggling to transform your vocabulary and to revisualize your dream and your goals. You haven't heard an answer from the finance group, but you did receive a message from them at lunch asking you to call them. You don't know whether that's good news or bad news. You aren't looking forward to the weekend anyway, so maybe you should call for the answer right now so you can deal with all the setbacks or negatives or whatever you call them all at once.

As you reach for the phone, it rings. The news is not from the finance group, but from a client you've been freelancing for. He likes your software so much he wants to convert his whole system to it, putting you in the black for the next few months. You hang up on a high, excited to end a tough week with good news. It's magical thinking not to make that call to the finance group, but your Mind's Eye decides magical thinking is allowable at this point because you need a positive weekend in which to regroup, mend your safety net, do contingency planning, and get your head back together. Your Mind's Eye decides that going through this process on a high, which is now possible if you don't make that phone call, is a necessary boost. Whatever you learn on Monday, you'll be able to deal with it better. So it says, "Let's just assume that the news from them is good as well. We'll rebuild our strength and call them Monday."

You have a great weekend. On Monday you call to discover that they need one more piece of information, which you give them immediately because your energy is restored.

Magical thinking is okay if your Mind's Eye approves it.

By the same token, your Mind's Eye won't let you make a phone call that could give you bad news on your way into an important sales meeting. It preserves your performance level by keeping the blinders on. It would be self-sabotage to make that call before the meeting, and your Mind's Eye is ever vigilant against self-sabotage.

the impostor syndrome

The question, "What makes you think you're an authority?" is bad enough when someone else asks it of you. But it can be worse if you're constantly asking it of yourself. One of the mind's favorite tricks is to use logic to set logic aside. Logically, you've never produced a film before, so how can you hope to be a producer? Remember, I didn't say the Accountant was brilliant. Because, by the same logic, no one who's never produced a film before could be a producer. But at some point, every producer had never produced a film before. This *do-loop*, as it's called in computer language, has been formally identified as the "imposter syndrome."

The good news is that it's absolutely normal for you to feel like an impostor. Feeling like an impostor is a symptom that comes with exploring new territory. If you don't feel like an impostor, you aren't serious about your career transit. When John Scott Shepherd—now an AEI partner but then an AEI client and the writer of *Joe Somebody* (starring Tim Allen and Julie Bowen), *Life or Something Like It* (starring Angelina Jolie and Ed Burns)—first told me his idea for a script he later titled *Henry's List of Wrongs*, I was in New York. That evening I had a drink at the Plaza's Oak Bar with an editor, and pitched the story to her.

"That's the best idea for a novel I've ever heard," she said. I could sense the excitement in her voice.

I called John when I got back to my apartment. "You've got to write it as a novel first," I said, "not a screenplay."

"A novel? I can't write a novel. I've never written a novel."

"Neither has anyone else who's never written one before."

"Point taken."

Fifty pages later he called to say he was "into it," and "on a roll." Despite feeling like an imposter, *Henry* sold to New Line for $1.6 million and to Pocket Books as part of a three-book deal.

tricks you can play on your mind

One of the advantages of aging is learning that you can, eventually, outwit yourself. Your mind, though never satisfied, does become more or less predictable—and you can get around it when it's misbehaving.

Carl Sagan, in *The Dragons of Eden*, argues that our sharp auditory recall is a throwback to our reptilian mind, when the sense of hearing was all-important for survival. As human beings evolved, we survived through our thinking. Yet we don't take our thinking as seriously as what we hear, see, or smell. A mundane example is the practice of repeating out loud something we want to remember. Hearing our voice say the phone number, or spell the name, imprints it more securely in memory than just thinking the name or number. That's a mind trick.

Another version of the same trick is using your voice to activate sleeping portions of the mind. When you can't remember a name, tell yourself out loud: "I can't remember the name." This often instantly triggers recall.

Inventory the tricks you've successfully played on your mind, and keep track of each new effort to defeat self-sabotage. One of the most important tricks I discovered years ago has been consistently effective in avoiding those little depressions we call funks or slumps. I came to the conclusion that if I associated these depressions—lasting from one hour to two or three days—with something positive I might not dread them as much. I made a list of things I never took the time to do, including reading magazines and playing video games. I kept the list in a handy place and decided that whenever I felt depressed I'd take it out. I started looking forward to getting depressed, thinking that I'd finally get to catch up with the stacks and stacks of magazines that had accumulated—and also learn how to play the latest video game. I don't think I applied the list more than once. The little slumps simply stopped occurring. My Mind's Eye's scheme had outwitted whatever sabotage was going on between Visionary and Accountant.

accountant: We're up Shit Creek without a paddle.
mind's eye: No, we're up Shit Creek with many paddles.
writer: He said my script was "promising."
friend: You can't let one adjective ruin your entire life.

Nearly everyone who writes about remotivation and career change stresses the importance of becoming aware of the words you say to yourself and to others. Whoever said, "Sticks and stones may break my bones, but words can never hurt me," was trying to divert attention from the most potent weapons. Pain for pain, we're probably more hurt by words than by any other weapon we've created.

Redefining your vocabulary and choice of terms means recreating the world you live in to fit the image of your dream. Examine your own story carefully to discover those negative "iceberg" words that may be doing you in:

- "I'm afraid that . . ."
- "We have a real problem."
- "I don't see how . . ."
- "It's impossible to . . ."
- "Weird."

In your career transit, you are defining and designing your life; don't forget to redesign your language. Your language defines your experience.

WORD TRANSFORMATION CHART

BAD WORDS	NEUTRAL WORDS	TYPE C WORDS
Anxiety	Uncertainty	Elation
Delusion	Illusion	Vision
Rejection	Pass	Open Door
Problem, Crisis	Situation	Opportunity
The Rat Race	Routine	My Vocation
Mercurial	Flexible	Spontaneous
I'm Quitting	I'm Stalled	I'm Regrouping
Impossible	Difficult	Interesting
Fear	Concern	Challenge
Failure	Stall	Learning Curve
Impediment	Consideration	Challenge
Defeat	Setback	Turning Point
Worry	Concern	Issue
Blame	Responsibility	Credit
Confused	Uncertain	Reassessing
Weird	Weird	Weird

There's nothing right or wrong about this chart; it's personal to me, as yours will be to you. When you get good at transforming your own vocabulary, you'll even begin seeing words differently. One particularly dark day, I forced myself to go to a meeting despite being on the edge of despair about whether I'd ever make it in this "crazy business." The meeting was inspiring, encouraging, and lifted my spirits immeasurably. I came out to discover a note on the windshield of my car. The note, in writing as jagged as it was sincere, said, "YOU ARE ON A ONE-WAY STREET!"

I'd been too upset to read my newspaper horoscope that morning, and had missed my fortune cookie for breakfast, so I immediately took this as a further sign that I was heading in the right direction—that my dream was within reach. When I got into the car and turned on the ignition, I noticed that I was facing traffic heading toward me in both lanes.

"I get it," I finally said. The note meant I was literally on a one-way street. Duh. I carefully backed into a driveway, to turn back with the flow of traffic, wondering whether my unconscious was issuing warnings again.

the never-satisfied mind

I was taught to be a perfectionist, but in a practical way. One hundred percent is the goal, but we aim for it with the foreknowledge that we're human and will never reach 100 percent, or if we do, we'll maintain it only temporarily.

Yet 100 percent is a better goal than 88 percent, because if 88 percent is your goal you'll never hit 90 percent. So 100 percent is a better goal as long as you understand that goals are, almost by definition, unreachable because the enterprising goal-seeker will have set a second goal by the time he accomplishes the first. If your goal is to finance a $30 million film, by the time you've closed your deal for $28.6 million, you'll be so busy planning your $75 million dollar film you won't be upset that you fell short on the earlier one by $1.4 million.

But the 100 percent standard is used by the Accountant as a superb sabotage mechanism. The Accountant uses the argument of "quality versus quantity." "Yes, I know you could rush to production with this new Visionary script. But a million things can go wrong with it down the road and it's better to troubleshoot them all before you make an enormous laughingstock of yourself with an equally enormous liability. Let's do a quality job." So the Accountant proceeds to supervise an endless troubleshooting expedition that tunes, fine-tunes, and re-tunes the script to the point that it's no longer recognizable; or until someone else goes public with the same story. "But I want it to be 100 percent perfect," the Accountant argues when the Mind's Eye scolds it. "We'll settle for 98 percent," replies the Mind's Eye, realizing that such a compromise is required if we're going to reap the benefits of the Visionary's great idea and escape from development hell.

Without losing the spirit of the quest for excellence, the perfectionist, also known as the judge or the critic, must be tamed if you are to accomplish your goals, objectives, and dreams. How do you know when to stop fine-tuning? You don't. Rewrites can go on indefinitely. You set a deadline, beyond which you will cease fine-tuning and begin preproduction.

bridling the imagination

albert einstein: Imagination is more important than knowledge.
pablo picasso: Everything you can imagine is real.
atchity: Imagination is the Type C's best friend—and worst enemy.

The Type C mind is constantly troubled by imagination, that Visionary breeding ground. As the Accountant uses perfection to sabotage progress, the Visionary never ceases to cast images on the Mind's Eye's screen. The damned thing just won't stop, like the little old lady in the shoe.

At one point I was determined to learn to take naps, just to get away from it all, and so I could stay up later and get up earlier without losing what was then left of my mind. I'd never been able to nap on airplanes, in cars, or even in the comfort of my own bed. I remembered that my mother was a champion napper, able to nap even in the midst of a lagging conversation. Her naps ranged in duration from several seconds to an hour, and she always awakened refreshed. So I called her for advice.

"Mom, I'm ready to get serious about napping. What's your secret?"

She'd been waiting all my life for this question. "I just imagine I'm a stick of butter, slowing melting on the stove. And then I melt into sleep."

"Great," I said. "I'll try it."

She called a few days later to ask how it had gone.

"It was a complete disaster," I said. "First I imagined the butter on the butter dish. Then it started melting. Then it started spilling over the sides of the dish onto the griddle, then down into the hole into the oven. Then the oven filled with black smoke, and the kitchen filled with smoke, until I could smell the smoke. . ."

She interrupted me. "You know you've always had an overactive imagination," she said. "You're too intense."

How do you quiet an overactive imagination? By telling it to shut up. I'm serious. The Type C's Mind's Eye has the authority and power to say, "Go away," to that agitated and unruly Visionary who won't stop yammering. That's what discipline is all about. You say to yourself (that is, your Mind's Eye says to your Visionary): "That's enough out of you today. Your ideas are great, but we're about to go offline and we'll check with you tomorrow." Or you find something else to do with your mind, like reading, until the yammering diminishes. It's a question of who's to be master. The very same mind that's been causing you all the trouble can be a wonderful co-worker once your Mind's Eye is the ringmaster.

eliminate self-doubt

atchity: How do you manage not to take your situation seriously?
friend: I just refuse to internalize every fucking problem I've
created for myself.

One of the Mind's Eye's first tasks is the elimination of the constant self-questioning that sooner or later institutionalizes itself as
self-doubt. The functional Type C runs a daily search-and-destroy
mission to eliminate the negative influences that lead you to question what you're doing. Living in dread of the end of the world
is narcissistic self-involvement instead of the kind of positive self-
investment it takes to make dreams come true. People with much
less going for them than you have succeeded in living peacefully
within their dreams, fulfilling their potential. Lack of self-confidence
is everyone's enemy—from the most consistent losers to the most
successful winners. But acting from lack of self-confidence is unnec-
essary, and an impediment to your forward progress.

Blame is also a waste of time. There's nothing you can do
about the mistakes you've made in the past, and spending valuable
time blaming yourself for them is just as futile as spending time
blaming others. Whatever happened, just move forward. One of
my clients had an enormous breakthrough when he decided that
his entire past life was a swamp in which he, an alien en route to a
bright new planet, had just landed temporarily. He determined to
regard the swamp simply as a given he had to operate on while
collecting what he needed to complete his voyage to the bright
new planet. Any time spent probing the swamp, he decided, was
wasted. He's been able to steal vast amounts of time simply by
refusing to look backwards.

In the same family of time-devourers, indecisiveness ranks
high. It's not a vice for most Type Cs, but it creeps into the lives of
some to throw them into a tailspin that swallows up weeks and
months. There are two kinds of good decisions: good decisions,
and bad decisions. A bad decision is almost as good as a good one
because, once made, we quickly learn that it is bad and are able to

begin the self-correcting process. The truly bad decision is the one that's postponed—because no self-correction, and consequently no forward movement, occurs. Learn to make the best decision you can with the facts at hand, review it for a predetermined amount of time, then put it into action, trusting yourself to correct errors in judgment as soon as you recognize them.

how often do i reevaluate?
harry truman: If you can't stand the heat, get out of the kitchen.
atchity: Get out of the kitchen just long enough to regain your appetite —but don't let the beans burn!

The Type C personality in career transit reevaluates every day. But reevaluation is not the same as indecisiveness. Let's call it instead "review and adjustment" of the game plan for the sake of confirming its validity and improving its focus based on new data. The important thing to remember is that you reevaluate your objectives before you reevaluate your goals, and you reevaluate your goals before you reevaluate your dream. If you find yourself constantly reevaluating your dream, you haven't yet made the commitment. Dreams are costly, and should not be pursued without the certainty that they are desired with your whole being.

One of the positive side effects of this daily reevaluation is that it automatically turns the anxiety you're feeling into that productive elation you now recognize as the natural result of your commitment to your goal. Getting out of the kitchen is a vacation from the center of the storm, where it's sometimes impossible for you to maintain your perspective. In the midst of the woods, you're so blinded by the thick trees of detail that you've forgotten which way is forward and which is backwards. Vacations allow you to escape being done-in by the details that preoccupy you in the kitchen's heat. You get out long enough to reevaluate, refocus, regroup your energies so that you can come right back into the heat refreshed, ready to cook again, hungry for your dream to continue.

concentration

The label on your career transit says, "Concentrate." As in tennis, the only way to win comes from keeping your eye on the ball.

At another turning point, I called my French–Louisiana Uncle Wilbur, who'd always been chief counselor in the family, to explain that I hadn't spoken with him for ages because I'd been "under the gun." He asked me enough specific questions to assess that my state of mind was quite fragile, too fragile to risk on conversations that might prove negative. We managed to visit through jokes and ended the phone call quickly. But a few days later, I received a wonderful card from him:

> I know you have been going through some trying times. Hopefully things will come all together soon. Please don't ever give up, as long as there is one small ray of hope. Like a good captain, stay on your ship and keep the sails up and ready. The breeze you need to touch your sails may be just a calm moment away, and may soon come to blow all your dreams into reality.

You are in the troubled straits of your Type C career transit, straits you've never navigated before. Bad enough that the cliffs are jagged and erratically jutting into the narrow waterway. Bad enough that there are lethal rocks hidden beneath the surface. Suddenly you find yourself, hands already blue-knuckled on the wheel, in a torrential downpour. Visibility is reduced to zero. You can't even see the surface of the water, much less the cliffs, much less the surface distortions caused by the submerged rocks. Then, your ship's compass is shattered by lightning. What do you do?

As tempting as it may be, jumping ship is most likely a terrible idea. You've gone so far now, it's easier to proceed than to abandon ship or turn back. The only logical thing to do is to maintain composure in the present, keep your hands firmly on the wheel, follow your instincts about the movements of the ship and the storm—and simply do the best you can. That's what being the captain of your dream is all about.

dream work

joseph campbell: Myth is public dream; dream is private myth.
atchity: Let's take our dreams public.

The Type C personality engaged in a heroic quest into the unknown country of career transit is living his private myth every day. It stands to reason that he should discover it directly by getting in touch with his dreams. How can your own unconscious not be useful to you? The brain is an image factory that never stops processing images: receiving them, storing them, recombining them, remembering them sometimes, forgetting them often, creating them, sending them back out again in a perpetual motion kaleidoscope.

Rather than puzzling over their meaning and allowing an unresolved feeling to nag you and force you to ignore your dreams, you can consult with your dreams for corroboration of your mission in life as well as for the answer to specific questions you have. This practice was known to the Greeks and Romans as "dream incubation." These ancients built temples where people would go to spend the night specifically for the purpose of consulting the gods of sleep and dream.

It was about two years into my career change when I spent the weekend at Gayle Delaney's and incubated the dream of the serpents. The incubation question was, "Am I doing the right thing?" Though I had just finished producing sixteen films, my financial situation seemed worse, not better. The problems were bigger, the solutions seemed as out of reach as they had before the deal was finally made. The first night's dream was something like this:

I'm on a ledge high up on a cliff wall, in pain, realizing I'm afraid of heights (for some reason, this recurring dream always reveals my fear of getting down, never of going up). I look up the cliff and see that the wall

between me and the top is all broken glass. I can't go up. I
look down and see that the cliff below is also broken glass.
No wonder I'm in pain. What to do? Going down would
be as painful as going up. Then I look at the ledge on
which my bleeding feet are standing, and realize it's covered with broken glass as well.

Was this a helpful dream? It was so brief a vision it seemed
insignificant.

The next morning, at breakfast, Gayle wanted to hear what
I had dreamed. I told her. She helped me realize that the dream
was, in fact, very significant. The only thing hopeful and positive and firm in the dream was my choice. I had chosen a
painful climb. Going down made no sense because it offered
only more pain with no reward. Standing still made no sense
for the same reason. Climbing to the top, through whatever
pain lay in wait, was the only alternative. As I do for my clients,
Gayle played the role of the Mind's Eye for me, sorting out the
meaning of this dream that seemed to encapsulate my
Accountant's anxieties.

The next night I dreamed that I was on an immense football
field, dwarfed by the giant players marching back and forth
against me. I had no idea what I was doing on the field: I wasn't
a football player. I was wearing the uniform of a soccer player,
not protected, as the giants were, by padding. Yet I managed to
dodge in and out of them, tricking the ball along as I went. Gayle
led me to interpret this dream by asking me first how I felt when
I woke up.

I told her I felt great. I was on a strange playing field in this
new film business I'd entered. Although I wasn't equipped like the
giants on the field, I was able to survive and make my way
through the game because I had other skills that were useful. I was
feeling like an impostor, in other words, precisely because in a
very real sense I *was* an impostor—going where I'd never gone
before. The best thing about the dream was its reminder that I was

on a playing field, playing a *game*. I had chosen my career change. No one was forcing me to have the problems I was having. If I could give myself perspective, by accepting my Mind's Eye's definition of what I was doing as a game, the pain might become more bearable. It was simply a matter of understanding the rules, knowing the objectives of the game, and using what skills I'd developed in my previous career to play as well as possible at any given moment.

Sometimes I employ a local hotel as my incubation temple. I used to make a practice of spending New Year's Eve alone at a new hotel in Los Angeles each year, taking only my journals with me to end the old year with reflection and to begin the New Year with resolve. Before going to sleep, I would ask my dreams for a vision of how I was doing.

meditation

john lennon: Life is what happens while we're making other plans.

zen: Do not look for the way. You are already there.

atchity: You have to come home often to appreciate the journey.

Sooner or later, people committed to changing themselves as a way of life turn to meditation of one sort or the other as an aid to "being there," being centered and present in the full intensity of your chosen life. No matter how complicated the various gurus make it seem, its bottom-line value is that it stills the mind.

More specifically, meditative breathing quiets the Accountant's constant shuttling of worry-beads, back and forth on his abacus, and the Visionary's screams of delighted discovery. The inner voices that never stop jabbering do stop during successful meditation, allowing your Mind's Eye to rise from the battlefield and find the tranquility of perspective. David Richo's *How to Be an Adult* offers a clear and simple guide to meditation that is well suited to the Western mind. A fifteen-minute meditation session in the middle of the typically crazy entrepreneurial day can do wonders for setting you back on course. But one successful Type C I know meditates just by looking out the window each morning before beginning her day.

the type c's astronomical event horizon
kenneth burke: Mankind is huddled together, nervously loquacious, at the edge of an abyss.
atchity: And what if the black hole is inside me?

Director Mort Ransen and I were talking about the weird life of the entertainment world one evening. One of its frustrations, he grumbled, is that its "event horizon" is "astronomical." I asked him to explain. He was referring to the moment at which matter either escapes from or disappears into a black hole—the black hole being failure, the escape being success. But so few tangible successes occur in the Type C's life: an acquisition deal actually closing, a finance deal actually closing, a star actually committing to a start-date while the financing is still available. A film finally being shot. A film finally being released. The rest is chatter and disappearances. The rest is straining your eyes at the telescope, trying to convince yourself that you will see a new constellation forming if you concentrate hard enough and long enough.

If your career transit has similar characteristics, don't forget that the event horizon began as your dream; the astronomical chart is your chart, your vision of what you could be. You've seen a possible future and begun behaving as if that future were real. Before long, people start catching the spirit and moving toward that future with you. From time to time, the future looms on the horizon—sometimes as shadow, sometimes with almost tangible substance. When you perceive it as shadow, you feel the depths of despair; when you feel its presence clearly, an unimagined elation washes over you. It may help to keep in mind the business principle: *No news means no news.* Don't make things worse by imagining what's not there. One of the systems I've invented to provide some sort of radar coverage of the event horizon is recording in my day-runner

green lights and red lights, positive events in green ink and
negative events in red. On a typical day during my transition,
five green lights occurred and generally no more than one red
light. Now a red light occurs, at most, once a month! A green
light is defined as a good sign that I'm making progress toward
a particular objective. A red light is an event that makes an
objective appear to be no longer possible. I've learned even *that*
isn't true: Red lights are opportunities, and I've learned to
concentrate on them until I see what they offer. Green lights
for me include:

- Financier agrees to do "offering" for a film
- A book by one of our Writers Lifeline clients sells after
  a year of hard work
- AEI signs a new client who's in demand by other man-
  agers or agents
- A studio attaches a great writer to one of our projects
- A network green-lights a client's TV series
- We sell a client's novel at auction

These are my red lights:

- A distributor refuses to give a quarterly accounting
- A publisher cancels a client's book
- One of our primary partners loses his financing
- I find out an ally is really an enemy

Recording these green lights and red lights as you transform your
vocabulary becomes increasingly encouraging. You see that the
greens are winning, partly because you're transforming setbacks
into challenges, delays into opportunities. The distributor's refusal
is a challenge that you'll meet more than once along the way.
Here's the chance to deal with it. Discovering the truth about an
erstwhile ally gives you a chance to reevaluate how you choose
allies in the first place.

Take credit for the fact that the entire process wouldn't be occurring if it weren't for your daring—if it weren't for your dream and your determination to pursue it. The dream will never come true if you stop believing in it. You are its sole and sufficient creator, and destroyer. If you continue, you can deal with whatever occurs on the event horizon.

how do you measure success?

Dealing with this frustrating event horizon really forces you to reevaluate your definition of success. Wouldn't it be a shame if you created your dream world out of elements unique to you, then failed to enjoy it because you were measuring it by someone else's standards? If you are in a difficult new career, where financial success comes rarely and only with extraordinarily good luck added to outstanding performance, don't make the mistake of measuring your success by where you now stand financially.

If this is a creative career, measure your success by your creative accomplishments; and yes, survival may be chief among them. You may not have made money on your first film, but it has your name on it. It's a "credit;" you're in the ballpark. Only three buyers asked to see your script, and all three passed on it, but now their doors are open, and you're in business. More than anything else, measure your success by the satisfaction that you feel and the recognition accorded you by others, sometimes grudgingly, that you are "doing your thing" and "following your bliss."

I know of no better definition than that of Thomas Carlyle, who defined success as "continual progress toward a worthy goal."

ups and downs

laurence sterne: There must be ups and downs, or how the deuce should we get into valleys where Nature spreads so many tables of entertainment.

atchity: I don't want to lose my humility.

best friend: Yeah, you do. You can't wait.

Maybe I like actual roller coasters because my life is a virtual roller coaster. "If one advances confidently in the direction of his dreams," Henry David Thoreau said in *Walden*, "he will meet with a success unexpected in common hours." The elations are indeed outstanding, the lows harrowing.

Once self-mastery gets him up and running, the entrepreneur meets with moments of success each and every day—finding a new corner to cut, handling a difficult phone call with style, deferring an impossible payment, finding a way to reduce costs. Let's make sure that we learn to recognize these moments, to savor them, to learn from them. Remember that success is in *process*, not in product or result.

Mastering the downgrades is obviously an important key to making your Type C behavior your greatest success. After all, the positive thing about being down is that you have nowhere to go but up. You know you will go up. Part of your mind—your Mind's Eye—knows it. So, if necessary, get into being down, remembering the line from *King Lear*: "The worst is never so long as we can say, this is the worst." When all else fails, embrace depression and bottom out with a preconstructed safety net. As the phoenix would say, "Once more, dear friends, into the ashes!"

Why are things so difficult? Because you've chosen a difficult path to challenge yourself, and to expand your potential. You are building character during these down cycles, character that will serve you well when you are on your way up again, and when you have reached the plateau you're dreaming of. Proof of this is what often happens to those who get lucky and experience precocious success. All too often they don't know what to do with it, blow it all, and find themselves without the resilience of character to make a comeback. So count yourself lucky when things go sour from time to time. It's your dream making sure you're worthy of it.

The down cycles are often simply reminders that you can't control everything. You can only move the ball toward the basket when it's in your court. You have little control over others. Letting go of the pretense that you're in control all the time is a huge step forward. When something unplanned occurs, take it as a sign that there are powers greater than you in charge and that it's all right to allow them to move you instead of your constantly attempting to move them. Because you've relied so much on planning, you will begin to *relish* the unplanned.

9

dealing with people:
family, spouses, best friends, ex-friends, associates, winners, losers, saviors, naysayers, white knights, black knights, clay gods, and the little red hen

shakespeare: The friends thou hast, and their affection tried/Grapple them to thy soul with hoops of steel.
atchity: The "friends" you had, their affection getting strained, replace those hoops with elastic bands. Be only with people with whom you can be yourself.

Nothing is more important to the career transit Type C than maintaining a positive support group. Without it, chances are you'll find yourself burning out and, unlike the phoenix, having no strength to rise from the ashes. Type C career transit success involves redefining all the people in your life by reference to your dream. They fall into three categories: good guys, bad guys, and guys who'd better declare themselves before you place them in the bad guy category. A good guy, by Visionary definition, is a family member, spouse, or friend who tells you to "Go for it!" and who reminds you to believe in yourself, reassuring you that you have the strength to overcome the problems you've freely chosen.

One businessman I interviewed focused his reaction to my question about his "darkest hour" on the support he got from his wife and family. At the time of the savings and loan collapse, he was deeply involved in real estate development:

Q: What was your darkest hour as an entrepreneur?
A: In 1990, the United States entered a major financial

155

crisis and the savings and loans were being taken over by the FSLIC [later called the Resolution Trust Corporation (RTC), run by the Department of the Treasury]. When they took over, they took away all my financing because they wouldn't assume contracts I had with banks to give my projects loans. I was stupid enough to believe this was just a hiccup in the system, so I used all my working capital—millions of dollars. The RTC would not allow other banks to refinance my projects. It wiped out the working capital that it had taken me twenty years to build up. I watched millions of dollars go down the drain.

Q: How did you feel about it as it was happening?

A: I didn't believe it was happening at first. I always believed I was at the top. I had confidence in the system, and never believed the system would fail me. But when I had to relieve my staff of their duties, I finally saw the light—or, I should say, the darkness. I felt completely alone, except for my wife and family. I never shared my problems with anyone else; though they had to know something was going on when we sold our multimillion-dollar house.

Q: What was your darkest vision during that time?

A: Not having a place to live, a place to keep my family intact. I never told anybody I feared that. I never told anybody I was afraid of anything. I did tell them it was the most humbling experience I'd ever had. I never worried about money; I always just focused on what I needed and how to get it.

Q: How did you move forward?

A: I have to say it was primarily through the support of my wife and kids, and their inspiration and motivation. They helped me reach the decision that if I did it once I could do it again. Through reorganizing my company I found another opportunity, got investors to believe in it again, and was able to rebuild the financing. I started buying the value-diminished assets back at major discounts, which enabled me to complete projects and sell them at below-market and begin repaying my debt—and along the way developed a new avenue of building nonperforming assets.

Q: What did you learn in retrospect?

A: Be stable. Be consistent. Don't change your way of life. Basic fundamentals really didn't change so I went back to those fundamentals. I traded my mansion for a $15 million debt, moving into a $300,000 house. The spiritual and mental way of life I didn't change, though I was forced to change my physical way of life. The turnaround took five years, 1990–1995, after which I moved back into a million-dollar house in the same city.

Q: What advice would you give people from your experience?

A: Believe in yourself. Take care of the people you love the most and who love you the most. Do not change your way of life. I always say that the epitaph I'd like on my grave is, "Here lies a man who reached his goals without violating the rights of others."

My friend had a clear vision of who the good guys in his life were, and he knew when to accept their support. When he "failed," they were there for him, providing him with the self-confidence the world had tried to strip away. That's what good guys are, for the entrepreneur. Bad guys are those who are worried about the decision you're making, and who never let go of their worried warnings, even when you are years into the transition. Often, the bad guy liked what you were before you made the switch. You were a good professor, so why are you sabotaging yourself by changing careers?

Unfortunately, the bad guy can be your father or mother, your child, your spouse, or your longtime friend. Weeks before I announced my resignation from Occidental College, I held a cocktail party at my home for nearly a hundred people. It was a kind of unofficial sayonara party to mark my transition. At the height of the party, an older professor who had been a close friend through the years came up to me and said, "Well, how does it feel to be an immoral businessman?"

"Exactly how it felt to be an immoral professor," I should have replied but didn't. The question floored me because it came from someone I very badly wanted to keep in my "good guy" set.

I once opened a UCLA seminar on career change for actors and actresses by asking, "What's the question you most hate to hear at cocktail parties, and how do you answer it?" The first actress said, "The question I hate most is, 'When are you going to move back to Detroit and take a job with the post office?'"

"How do you answer it?" I asked.

"I usually burst into tears and leave the party."

I told her I understood, then moved on to the second actress. She said the question she hated most was, "What have you been in big lately that I've seen?"

Her answer was, "The Pacific Ocean."

The difference between these two career-transit Type Cs is that one had figured out how to defend herself against the bad guys, and the other had not. Sticks and stones are not your enemy, but casual words that come from friendly people are often the toughest obstacles of career transit.

One day, driving through the San Joaquin Valley back to Los Angeles, I had time to think about something very sad and resolve my future actions regarding it. Two particular friends had been calling recently, and I didn't want to call them back. In one case it always meant making nice on the phone, then sidestepping the suggestion of setting a specific date for getting together. In the second case, even the phone call wasn't so nice. The second friend always managed to make digs, and I always reacted negatively to them, and the call always ended badly.

The first had a pattern of inviting me to dinner in his faraway neighborhood (because he couldn't drive), which I always paid for (because it had long ago been established between us that I was better off), at a restaurant of his choice (because he had a list of dietary restrictions), while I listened to his latest tales of woe. I found myself thrilled when he'd reach only my answering machine, and equally thrilled when I reached his. In the interest of friendship, I continued seeing him, even though each time I did I felt scared. Scared by the "There but for the grace of God go I" syndrome. In my own darkest imagination, I had seen myself as down and out as this friend, and it didn't create a positive reality for me to witness exactly how down and out that was.

I always drove home from our get-togethers asking myself what distinguished the two of us—I a cock-eyed dreamer determined to create a better future, and he someone hoping I would create that future right away so I could help him. I finally realized that both "friendly associates" were what Judith Viorst calls "necessary losses" and I needed to govern myself accordingly. In the next few years, I allowed one to drift away without returning his calls, and confronted the other with the truth that our lives had simply gone different ways. Eventually, we found more comfortable ways of communicating, mostly by postcard.

temporary friends versus life friends

Perhaps nothing is more distressing in career change than the inevitable necessity of leaving behind people you regarded, in your previous career, as "life friends." One of the problems is that, in the rush of initial enthusiasm, we don't bother to define the concept of friends very carefully. Life friends are the ones who are left when nothing else is working out, who stick with you when you're at your lowest, and when you're at your worst. I'm happy to say that I'm fortunate to have a few friends who have become even closer during the long career change I've undertaken. They are life friends.

The friends who've fallen behind weren't false friends; they were temporary friends, mistaken at the time for life friends and now seen in retrospect for what they were. There's nothing wrong with leaving temporary friends behind. Should you run into them, your greetings will be warm, your memories mutually endearing, your affection apparently intact. But the feeling of dissatisfaction and self-questioning you experience as you walk away from such a chance encounter cries out for attention. It's normal. It happens to all of us, as those who make it a habit to attend high school or college reunions can attest. The dissatisfaction doesn't stem from the present situation; it stems from your past being less important than your future.

petrarch: I have learned that complaints are useless, that nothing avails but patience in the things we cannot change.
atchity: Okay, but would you mind a little whining?

Motivational experts tell you, "Don't complain!" I would add, "Just find someone to whine to when you need to." Your life friend is that someone. When you whine, he says, "That's okay. I know it's tough. But you're doing great. You've chosen these problems, and you're getting through them." The person who responds to your whining with warnings and, "I told you so" or "That's just what I was afraid would happen," is not being a friend to the entrepreneur dedicated to pursuing his dream.

negative people and positive people

The pressures of career change are so great that you can't afford to spend your time or energy with negative people, which is what some of the temporary friends have become in your new life. If a friendly associate from the past falls into that category, sooner or later one of two things will happen: You'll either leave him behind once and for all, or you'll be dragged back into the past. You need every bit of positivism you can muster to continue marching forward into your dream world. Marsha Sinetar (*Do What You Love, The Money Will Follow*) admonishes:

To the extent that we accept our own greatness, the mission and charter for our own life, we want to work against anything—either external (in society or through the actions and efforts of others) or internal (our own "enemies within")—that would hold us back.

Those who aid and abet your dream are the positive people, whether they do it through psychological support or financial investment. Those who counter your dream—questioning it, blocking it, resenting it, demanding explanations for it—are enemies of the dream. Recognizing them as such allows you to do the right thing, finding a humane way of parting with them when you can't transform them into a positive force in your life.

Every transaction between people is a contract of some sort, and a contract must be a two-way street or it doesn't last very long. You give a dollar to a homeless woman on the corner as you go into the Blockbuster video store. She smiles and thanks you. You feel better about yourself. The contract is minimal, but it's clear nonetheless. The next day, she's there again. You're torn. Another dollar for another smile? Maybe. But as days go by, if the smile is all you're getting, you feel uncomfortable about the outgoing dollars. You'd rather contribute to a charity where something definite is done to improve the future prospects of the recipients. The woman on the corner isn't making discernible progress from your dollar. The people who loiter around your bandwagon can be divided into those who help it roll and those who slow it down so they can get on. The ones you define as positive are the former; those you think of as negative are the latter.

"Missionary work" is something we all do pro bono, nurturing and supporting those less fortunate than ourselves. But when missionary work becomes so all-consuming that it interferes with your dream, you're kidding yourself about its altruistic nature. You're avoiding your own potential, sabotaging the Visionary within. Choose your missions carefully. Select activities that allow you to give back to the world without expecting immediate return, and concentrate your charitable instincts on them instead of diffusing them throughout your life.

Just like the advice for dating—"It doesn't get any better!"— the advice for dealing with people in business is, "follow your initial instincts." If you don't like or trust or feel good about someone, and have confirmed this feeling with a second opinion, don't do business with him. Assume that there are enough good, positive people in the world who'll recognize the value of your dream; and realize that making deals with the wrong ones just wastes your time. If you're free of the bad guys, the good guys have a chance to meet you. If you're tied up with the bad guys, the good guys deal with others.

A client once realized that she'd never be able to work on her novel during November and December, because the holidays always brought her together with her mother, who constantly pointed out that she could barely spell, much less write. Knowing she had a deadline to meet, I asked her, "What are you going to do about it?" Rather than allowing her to answer, I urged her to think about it and tell me at our next meeting. When she came in the next week, she said, "I can't believe I did it."

"What did you do?"

"I told my mother I wasn't coming for the holidays."

"Did you tell her why?"

"No, she didn't ask."

She remained true to herself, avoided her mother, and finished her novel by January. Of course she experienced the ghost of guilt. But I pointed out to her that experiencing that was preferable to experiencing the self-disgust she normally felt when she put herself in her mother's negative sphere of influence.

When you take such self-protective actions to nurture your dreams, giving them priority over your past problems, amazing things occur. Her mother started getting interested in her book, and managed to ask about it in a positive way. When she realized my client's dedication was strong enough to confront even her enormous influence, the mother came around to her daughter's side. She had finally acknowledged the strength of her Type C daughter's dream, and realized that she didn't want to be relegated to the negative column. She decided to join the bandwagon.

After giving a seminar at Villanova, I encountered one of my Yale professors whom I hadn't seen in twenty years. Over slices of his exquisite homemade wheat-berry bread, he told me he was concerned for his daughter, a struggling actress in New York. He had been supporting her, but was beginning to think he should urge her to do something practical, since she was experiencing a very long dry spell. I advised him to withhold that advice, and instead to ask her if she still believed in her career. If she said, "Yes," he should express his undying support for her. "Not financial support," I added. "That's not required of you."

I explained to him that, for a Type C, unqualified emotional support is the lifeblood of daily renewal. When self-confidence flags, the support of loved ones provides a transfusion that gets you through your mood. If his daughter decides she's ready to give it up, he can support her in a more "practical" decision. But in the meantime he shouldn't worry about her examining the alternatives. The Type C's onboard Mind's Eye examines the alternatives proposed by his Accountant so thoroughly and so constantly that the Mind's Eye doesn't need to hear the recitation of practicalities from someone whose support for the dream is vital.

Once, during a particularly painful financial stage in my career transit, my mother, who had inspired me originally, and whose emotional, psychological, and financial support had filled in so many gaps over the years, fell into the pattern of becoming the bad guy. I had gone to Kansas City to visit a client who wanted to make the transition from the clothing industry (he was a "garment diverter," who'd made a small fortune intercepting brand-label shipments intended for one retailer and reselling them at a higher price to another). My mother wanted to know why this man had so much money. When I explained to her what he did to earn it, she said, "You know, you'd be good at doing that." Buzz . . . Wrong answer, Mom. It was my responsibility to correct her and set her back on my course. "What I need from you, Mom, is your support and encouragement. I am not going to starve to death. I would, in fact, prefer to starve to death than to do something other than my dream." Don't expect your positive support group to be perfect. They're human, like you, and allowed to falter once in awhile. Supporting you can be as exhausting for them as continuing the quest is for you.

Sometimes we need to give the people around us a chance to adjust to our dream. Friends are coming for the weekend unexpectedly. You're torn between putting in three hours on Saturday morning pursuing your dream, and entertaining your friends. You do the right thing, dragging them to Six Flags. They notice that you're grumpy. You may or may not admit why, but you certainly know: You'd rather be working on your dream. The friends pick up on your mood, its reasons, and feel guilty; the day deteriorates.

Or, your friends announce that they're coming. You tell them you're always delighted to see them and look forward to spending some time with them. "Meanwhile, I hope you guys can entertain yourselves Saturday morning. I've got some effect sketches to go over with my art director, and we're under a deadline."

"Are you sure we won't be imposing?" they ask.

"Not at all, if you don't mind my being out-of-pocket a few hours."

When they hear that you mean it, they say, "Hey, we're old enough to take care of ourselves. In fact, we'll sit around the pool while you're gone. Don't worry about us. We'll get lunch ready if you'd like . . . . We'd love to hear about your project when you get a chance." You feel good about their visit, and good about yourself. You've given them the opportunity to adjust to your dream world, to involve themselves in it by understanding. They feel good because you're accepting them into your new life without making them the bad guys.

You can also make use of the triadic mind to help transform the less-than-positive people around you into ones who will support your dream. Tell them about the Accountant, the Visionary, and the Mind's Eye. Ask them which part of them is responding the way they are. It's often their own desire to lead a Type C life that's underlying their negativity, and helping them become aware of it is sometimes all that's needed to alter their behavior. "Your Accountant is telling me that, isn't it?" you say. "I'll bet your Visionary would agree with me, if you'd just let me explain what I'm doing to your Mind's Eye." Since everyone experiences the

three voices to one extent or another, this will almost always get
their attention.

naysayers and grumbling soldiers

There was a grumbling soldier
Who grumbled all day long.
What wasn't was what ought to be—
What was was always wrong.

—James Whitcomb Riley

In avoiding those who don't recognize and affirm your ability to
attain your dream, don't confuse "grumbling soldiers" with
"naysayers." Some people always complain. It's just their nature.
You don't need their good mood; you need their assistance. Don't
expect them to change their nature just because you're suddenly
involved. But watch what people do instead of what they say. One
of my best Yale professors was a grumbling soldier, who nonetheless managed, in his thoroughness and precision, to be totally
inspiring when teaching a very difficult subject.

The naysayers, on the other hand, may be cheerful in
demeanor but their attitude sucks. You go to them for advice, and
they say, "You're so bright, I don't understand why you've gotten
yourself into this new career. Why don't you do something
easier?" You've encountered them before: They're the bad guys.

the limited marriage

I don't mean to suggest that you can't deal with the bad guys at
all. You take what you can get from them without marrying them,
and discard the rest. You tell them, "I didn't come to you for
career counseling I came to ask you a specific question." You
remain in control of the relationship.

My brother Fred has always said that even when someone is
eight-ninths bad, he can find one-ninth that's useful for advancing
business. But that approach means retaining your perspective, and

refraining from prematurely jumping into bed with someone you have less than a perfect response to. I call this the "limited marriage," and find it infinitely preferable to "full marriages" in business. Never throw your entire business lot in with one party. That's a sure way of sabotaging yourself, and abdicating your role as hero of your own Type C story. You have more control over your career transit if you have many alliances on individual projects and contracts and deals than if you have one "grand alliance." You are married to your dream. You are related to others whose dreams are compatible with yours, and who can therefore assist you in advancing your dream more rapidly, through their cooperation on a given objective of your operating plan, than you can advance it alone.

A corollary of the limited marriage principle is this: Seek the right kind of help from the right people on the right terms. It takes a while to figure out how to identify each of these categories. But once you do, you'll move forward with greater assurance and with greater integrity to your dream. If your instincts are telling you that the other person is a complete skunk, forget even a limited marriage. Follow the Cajun advice: "A skunk's territory ain't negotiatiable."

when to avoid the winners

I'd like to agree with the motivational experts who say, "Never avoid winners—not even when you're feeling down and out and know that being with them at the New Year's football games will make you feel worse." The theory being that, simply by faking the self-confidence to be with them, you actually are a winner. They'll recognize you're down, but they won't count you out.

Nonsense. This approach doesn't work when you're down. And you can expect to be down from time to time along the way, despite everything you do to control your mood and change your vocabulary. If you think that spending New Year's Day with the winners will set you back, interfere with your motivation, then by all means follow your instinct. Being with the winners and feeling like you're losing isn't good for anyone at the party. It takes enormous self-confidence to enjoy someone else's success when you're being beaten over the head by so many obstacles that all you can see are the wrong kinds of stars. If you're serious about making a career transit based on your dream, no one can expect you to be self-confident all the time. The important thing is simply to keep moving forward, even if that means taking occasional side trips to regain your sanity, and hiding out from the winners long enough to get your spirits back up.

Of course, what I've said earlier about going to meetings when you're feeling down applies here as well. When you do force yourself to hang out with those who've already attained their dream, even on a day when you see yours slipping over the horizon, fate has a way of encouraging you. Something will almost surely happen at the party, a contact you might never have otherwise made, a piece of information of incalculable value, a snatch of conversation that gives you the perspective you needed to go to the mountaintop to find. Try it, you'll see. Synchronicity always happens when you're pursuing your true path.

network only with the right people

"Networking," that buzzword of motivational seminars, may indeed be an essential part of career change, although it should be done with intelligence and caution, and never for the wrong reasons. Too many networking meetings are attended purely to socialize. Instead of helping the quest, they distract you from your objectives.

Nor will networking with the wrong people advance your quest. I spoke one evening at a women's support group in New Orleans, where the atmosphere was thick with intense networking. After my talk, one of the women asked me, "How much networking did you do in your career change?" I was surprised to hear my own answer: "Not much." I hadn't gone to seminars (except those I was giving), hadn't attended conferences, belonged to no support groups—although after a visit with Barbara Sher (*Wishcraft*) I longed

to have a support group that would really understand what
I was doing and could truly support me. But each time I'd been
moved to join one, I pulled back. Networking with the wrong
people is worse than not networking at all. I'd much rather read a
book.

There is one enormously wonderful suggestion: a "master
mind group," as defined by Napoleon Hill in his motivational
masterpiece *Think and Grow Rich.* The *mastermind* is a group of
people—three is ideal—who get together to support each other as in
"Together, we share a brain." One of the only rules of the mastermind group is this: Everyone must give unquestioned support.

Although I've had the pleasure of speaking at many productive,
positive groups, too many support groups support losing. That's
why any winners who manage to emerge from them stop
attending. Once, in Houston, I spoke at a Saturday morning
group. After my talk the group leader asked me what I'd thought
of the session.

"If you want my honest opinion," I said, "I thought your group
was in danger of becoming very depressing." He seemed surprised,
until I pointed out all the self-demeaning humor characterizing
the group's individual reports of their monthly progress.

"I see what you mean," he said. "How can we fix that?"

I suggested that the group adopt a rule that every report must
be a progress report, in which the individual first details the forward steps he's taken in the last month, and only after doing so be
allowed to lightheartedly explain what he had to overcome to
make that step.

The networking meeting that's typically useful is one in
which you can meet people who are farther along the road you're
taking than you are.

My networking, instead, was largely one on one. It entailed
reading books and corresponding with authors who interested me,
which has led to some wonderful letters and phone calls that have
been tremendously supportive; finding directories appropriate to
my business and searching them for any contacts I could use;

writing letters; and arranging introductions through friends. I've been lucky enough to have more than one mentor along the way. I heartily recommend that you find someone either to model yourself upon in your new enterprise, or to advise you as you reach for your goals, or both.

some general tips about networking

Do it in your own way. If you're not a social person but know that the party you're invited to will offer outstanding contacts, go to the party but be content with making only a single contact. Don't worry about working the room. I've never failed to make an interesting contact at a party, but I've never tried to make more than one—though sometimes I've made several. I feel more comfortable this way. Here are some more helpful tips:

- **Create a method for keeping track of your contacts and keeping them up-to-date by contributing something to their lives.** I send out *Door to Door*, a collection of favorite trivia and conversation and cartoons I gather throughout the year. When people don't receive it, they call me to find out why. I keep a computerized mailing list, and let my contacts know about a forthcoming film, book reading, or lecture.
- **Go to the top.** If you see something that interests you, find out who's in charge and write or call that person. This isn't always appropriate (sometimes you can receive vital insights from someone who's not at the top), but it's always a good idea to consider the "chief" as a first approach.
- **Identify the human interests of your network.** They are people, not opportunities. Eat with them, laugh with them, share their personal interests.
- **Realize that a small, vital network is more effective than a large, loosely organized group that you can't possibly keep up with.** For one thing, you can't

get to know a thousand people personally. But you can
get to know twenty or thirty.
* **Respect everyone's time**. Find ways of communicating
that make a response easy for them.
* **Don't be afraid to show your appreciation**. Send
notes, send flowers. Thank people for the favors they do,
in ways that respect who they are.
* **Be specific**. Don't waste your contact with a busy
person by simply asking for help without having any idea
what kind of help you're asking for.

bible: Ask and you shall receive.
atchity: Ask for advice. But ask the right people.

Self-reliance is essential to the Type C's career transit. But it
doesn't mean having no need for people. Stephen Covey (*The
Seven Habits of Highly Effective People*) calls the proper attitude
"interdependence" as opposed to "independence" or "depend-
ence." When you need help, and your own skills aren't sufficient,
don't avoid the resources around you. In the years of my career
transit, I've identified an informal group I call my advisers. We've
only had an official meeting once, at a particularly painful
economic turning point. Most of the time it's been a matter of
telephone advice and support.

I find that asking for advice is the most natural way of making
use of the human resources around me. It's the least intrusive to
the person on the other end of the line. You don't need to ask
him to save you, or to make a deal with you, or to give you a
break. Asking for advice allows him to be his best, and to do so
objectively. What your adviser has that you don't isn't money or
solutions or better product, but perspective.

Persist in casting your net out, sending out daily signals to find
those positive people who will help you reach the "Yes." I get the
best responses when I'm discouraged, yet still have the stamina to
make those calls or attend those meetings. Once life sees that

you're serious about your vision, she can't resist responding; and there's no greater seriousness than doing something even when you don't feel like doing it. Remember Ray Bradbury's exhortation: "Start doing more; it'll get rid of all those moods you're having." The most important thing you can do is make contact with the right people, relentlessly pruning away the negative as you forge and focus your positive network.

godfathers, saviors, white knights, the little red hen, and clay gods

When you're lucky enough to find a godfather or a godmother who shares your vision enough to support you with advice and contacts, don't make the mistake of enshrining that person on a pedestal with solid-gold status. Do not create a savior for yourself. If you need a savior, you're already past saving. Regarding a rescuing ally as a savior gives him too much power over your goals. His reward for the rescue should be specific, not general; and it should be tangible and immediate enough that ongoing gratitude toward him doesn't interfere with your freedom to continue moving toward the dream.

In the heroic quest you're undertaking through this career change, remember that you are and must remain the hero of your own story. You are "getting your story straight." No one else can do that for you.

I've always loved the fable, which my mother read to me repeatedly, of the "Little Red Hen" who wanted to bake bread. She made a survey of her barnyard friends and discovered that none of them were interested in helping her. They were too busy. Only her chicks wished her well. So she decided to do it all herself. Once the bread was in the oven, the aroma wafting across the barnyard, the friends began to gather around. But the Little Red Hen decided she was going to share the bread only with her chicks. The moral of this perhaps overly selfish story is that the only sure way to get what you want done is to do it yourself. How you deal with the "bandwagon effect" depends on your mood at the moment of victory. One successful Type C took the Little Red Hen's philosophy to the extreme. He dreamed of ending his career by building a castle on a high hill with a stonewall around it inscribed with the legend: "FUCK YOU GUYS!" Another spends an enormous amount of time finding charitable outlets for his money, figuring he would rather give it to worthy causes he himself chooses than to the IRS.

Anyone can play the role of ally, dragon, kindred spirit, or white knight. But no one else can fight your battles for you. If you see every helper as a white knight coming to your rescue, not only will you risk disappointment when that person turns out to be more interested in his own story than in yours, but you'll also have disempowered yourself by turning over the responsibility for your success to someone else. The disillusionment you experience when you recognize that your god has feet of clay is actually disappointment in yourself for having deified another human being. People who are regularly deified don't like it; it's dehumanizing to be a god.

"I used to hold you on a pedestal," one of my clients once told me. "Yes, and I never appreciated it," I said. In fact, nothing's surer to chase away a would-be ally than the feeling he gets that you're relying upon him too heavily. It's a sign that you aren't ready to be the hero of your own story yet.

10

failing forward

I was never afraid of failure; for I would sooner fail than not be among the greatest.—*John Keats*

I haven't failed; I've found ten thousand ways that don't work.—*Thomas A. Edison*

yogi berra: It ain't over till it's over.
atchity: It's over when you say it's over—never before.

Is it ever a good idea to wake up from the dream? To stop putting yourself through this torture? When you can't find even the tiniest morsel of hope to suck on, the dream is no longer sustainable, no longer worthwhile; but the deeper you get into your dream the better you get at finding hope.

If the dream no longer motivates you to seek the hope, it may indeed be time to slam the door shut so you can benefit from the Spanish proverb my sister Mary once sent me: "For every door that closes, a thousand doors open." The doors of possibility open only when the door of disappointment is firmly shut. Meanwhile, while you are still able to bear disappointment don't confuse it with failure; and don't confuse setbacks, down cycles, or depression with failure. Success is failing forward as quickly as possible. I remember a particularly tough time of transition, when I was trying to continue with one of my companies when everything seemed stacked against it. I asked a friend and investor to analyze the situation for me, and he gave me a day of his time to listen and do so—partly to protect his investment. When I was finished explaining the situation, he said, "You have no choice but to keep going."

"Why?" I wasn't sure if I was happy or sad to hear him say that.

"Because success is the fastest and surest way to untangle the mess you've gotten into. 'Giving it up' at this point, considering everything I've observed, is more complicated than 'going for broke.'"

It turned out he was right: I continued, and succeeded, and not only untangled the mess but was able to go on to others even more complicated. After his observation, at moments like this, I recall e.e. cummings' poem about the tightrope walker: "an artist, a man, a failure, proceed." Proceeding is what makes you an effective dreamer. According to George Kennan, the Caucasian mountaineers define heroism as "endurance for one moment more."

Here are some thoughts from one of the most amazing entrepreneurs I know. Once an attorney, he made the transition to telecommunications, then to magazines:

> **Q:** What was your darkest hour as an entrepreneur?
> **A:** The day of shutting down a failed business. The moment I realized the magazine had failed. It was exhausting. I was so tired I couldn't go on anymore. I realized we were done for; I had no ideas left. I also had no personal reserves left to keep going. Both financially and mentally I was tapped out.
>
> **Q:** How did you feel about it as it was happening?
> **A:** I felt disgusted with myself, and very self-deprecating as if, wow, what could I have done better, differently? Did I not do right? I was very down on myself.
>
> **Q:** What was your darkest vision during that time?
> **A:** That not only was the business shut down but that other investors would come after me legally and make my

life miserable going forward, and that would spread into family breakup and that I'd end up alone.

Q: How did you deal with it?

A: I took total responsibility, confronted the people I needed to confront, told them I'd done my best, and started over. I took a lot of heat in that process. Everyone else chose to vent every piece of their anger and frustration on me, which I decided to accept in exchange for defusing that anger to the point where I would not face lawsuits—which is exactly what happened. No one sued me. They just went away.

Q: How did you move forward?

A: Most importantly, I took time. Understanding there was no way I'd be healed by the following Monday, I gathered my internal strength and slowly put it back together—it took six months to get the mental state to go after something new. Severe debt restructuring and debt management. Bankruptcy might have been easier.

Q: What did you learn in retrospect?

A: I learned that I don't care what business it is, if you're not running it by the numbers, you're not running it. And I also learned that if you fail to plan, you plan to fail. If you go into something because you have a great idea and don't do the research to find out exactly how it works, create a written plan, marshal the resources necessary, and then execute that plan, you might as well as go get a job.

Q: What advice would you give people based on your experience?

A: If you're not truly passionate about engaging in a venture and prepared to make significant personal sacrifices, don't do it. If you are, be prepared to make the sacrifices and understand that, as bad as you think it's gonna be, it'll be twice as bad, twice as long, and twice as expensive.

Businesses fail for one of two reasons: (1) lack of capital; and (2) because people don't realize just how hard it going to be to succeed. If you lose, don't lose the lesson. Within victory lies the cause of defeat; within defeat lie the seeds for victory the next time.

Success experts agree that rejection and failure are, in fact, the keys to success. The friend interviewed above went on to become a widely recognized motivational speaker. All successful people have not only experienced rejection and failure, but have gotten good at thriving on them. "When I was a young man," George Bernard Shaw said, "I observed that nine out of ten things I did were failures. I didn't want to be a failure, so I did ten times more work."

My mother once came out to visit me in the middle of a development deal that had been dragging on for two years, its continued promise depending entirely on my efforts. Everyone around me thought I was crazy to continue investing my time, money, and energy in the project. I asked her if she too, thought I should give it up.

"Do you still have hope in it?" she asked.

"Yes." I said.

"Then you should continue," she said.

"Thanks, Mom. I needed to hear exactly that."

I continued, and the deal was eventually made. It's true that, as Bill Russell says, "It takes a winner to know when to change directions." But a winner will first try multiple readjustments before giving up the game. You can't win if you don't stay in.

Even if you decide it's time to hang it up on a particular project, leave the kitchen for a while before you implement your decision. Take a little vacation. You'll be surprised, until it's happened a few times, what's likely to occur. While you're away:

1. The decision you've been waiting for will be made; the project will come together
2. You re-motivate yourself more strongly than ever to continue

3. Or most rarely, you confirm your decision to hang it up, and feel like a mountain range has been lifted from your shoulders, freeing you to fly again

jugglers and tightrope artists

beckett: Do not come down the ladder. I have just taken it away.
atchity: Which leaves the Type C in a precarious position indeed.

The successful high-wire acrobat doesn't look down. The fine line between success and failure is a single misstep; and proceeding with a dangerous self-chosen career risks that failure at every turn. But you can't become a juggler if you're not willing to drop a ball. Improvement comes only by dropping them. A tightrope artist must be willing to risk a fall, as much as he strives to avoid it. Carl Jung observed: "Where there is a fear of falling, the only solution is to jump."

Think of all the money you've spent so far as part of your investment in yourself. The time to analyze the risk-reward ratio is after you've struck it rich. It's impossible to analyze it before then because you don't yet know the final numbers. Looking back at the money you've spent is something you can do from the luxury of the mountaintop. Looking back before you've reached the peak just makes you dizzy and threatens your focus as you climb.

Whatever occurs, in this great adventure that is your life, you will never want for dreams. If the dream that started with an outstanding logo and beautiful stationery has now become scrap paper, all is not lost. It's now part of your arsenal, and has educated your Mind's Eye to do a better job on the next dream.

Failure, for the Type C, comes in failing to steal the time you need to do what you dream.

confucius: The way out is through the door.
atchity: Every door you close firmly behind you gives you a new room to explore.

suggested reading

Atchity, Kenneth. *A Writer's Time: Making the Time to Write*, 2nd ed. New York: W. W. Norton & Co., 1995.

Atchity, Kenneth, with Chi-Li Wong. *Writing Treatments That Sell: How to Create and Market Your Story Ideas to the Motion Picture and TV Industry*, 2nd ed. New York: Owl Books/Henry Holt & Company, 2003.

Atchity, Kenneth, with Julie Mooney and Andrea McKeown. *How to Publish Your Novel: A Complete Guide to Making the Right Publisher Say Yes*. New York: Square One Publishers, 2005.

Bliss, Edwin C. *Getting Things Done: The ABC's of Time Management*. New York: Bantam Books, 1984.

Boldt, Laurence. *Zen and the Art of Making a Living: A Practical Guide to Creative Career Design*. New York: Penguin, 1999.

Branden, Nathaniel. *Honoring the Self: Self-Esteem and Personal Transformation*. New York: Bantam Books, 1985.

Campbell, Joseph. *Myths to Live By*. New York: Arkana, 1993.

Carlson, Richard. *Don't Worry, Make Money: Spiritual & Practical Ways to Create Abundance and More Fun in Your Life*. New York: Hyperion, 1997.

Clance, Dr. Pauline Rose. *The Imposter Phenomenon: When Success Makes You Feel Like a Fake*. New York: Bantam Books, 1986.

Cousins, Norman. *Anatomy of an Illness as Perceived by the Patient*. New York: Bantam Books, 1991.

————. *Human Options.* New York: Berkley Publishing Group, 1989.

Covey, Stephen R. *The Seven Habits of Highly Effective People.* New York: Simon & Schuster, 1990.

Delaney, Gayle M. *Living Your Dreams*, rev. ed. San Francisco: Harper & Row, 1996.

Epel, Naomi. *Writers Dreaming.* New York: Vintage Books, 1994.

Fisher, Roger, and William Ury. *Getting to Yes: Negotiating Agreement Without Giving In*, 2nd ed. New York: Penguin USA, 1991.

Frankl, Viktor E. *Man's Search for Meaning*, revised and updated edition. New York: PocketBooks, 1997.

Friedman, Meyer, M.D. Type *A Behavior and Your Heart.* New York: Fawcett Books, 1983.

Friedman, Meyer, M.D., and Diane Ulmer. *Treating Type A Behavior and Your Heart.* New York: Fawcett Books, 1985.

Gawain, Shakti. Creative *Visualization: Use the Power of Your Imagination to Create What You Want in Your Life.* San Rafael, Calif.: New World Library, 2002.

Gleick, James. *Chaos: Making a New Science.* New York: Penguin USA, 1998.

Goldberg, Herb, and Robert T. Lewis. *Money Madness: The Psychology of Saving, Spending, Loving, and Hating Money.* Stevens Point, Wisconsin: Wellness Institute, 2000.

Helmstetter, Shad. *What to Say When You Talk to Yourself.* New York: PocketBooks, 1990.

Hendricks, Gay, and Kathlyn Hendricks. *At the Speed of Life: A New Approach to Personal Change Through Body-Centered Therapy.* New York: Bantam Books, 1994.

Hill, Napoleon. *Think and Grow Rich.* New York: Fawcett Books, 1990.

Houston, Jean. *The Possible Human: A Course in Enhancing Your Physical, Mental, and Creative Abilities.* Los Angeles: J. P. Tarcher, 1997.

Iacocca, Lee, with William Novak. *Iacocca: An Autobiography.* New York: Bantam Books, 1986.

Jaynes, Julian. *The Origin of Consciousness in the Breakdown of the Bicameral Mind*. New York: Houghton Mifflin Company, 2000.

Kasl, Charlotte Davis. *Finding Joy: 101 Ways to Free Your Spirit and Dance with Life*. New York: Harper Perennial, 1995.

Keen, Sam, and Anne Valley-Fox. *Your Mythic Journey: Finding Meaning in Your Life Through Writing and Storytelling*. New York: Jeremy P. Tarcher, 1989.

Korda, Michael. *Power! How to Get It, How to Use It*. New York: Warner Books, 1991.

Kuhn, Robert Lawrence. *Dealmaker: All the Negotiating Skills and Secrets You Need*. New York: John Wiley & Sons, 1990.

Lakein, Alan. *How to Get Control of Your Time and Your Life*. New York: New American Library, 1996.

Mackay, Harvey, and Kenneth H. Blanchard, *Swim with the Sharks Without Being Eaten Alive: Outsell, Outmanage, Outmotivate, and Outnegotiate Your Competition*. New York: Fawcett Books, 1996.

May, Rollo. *My Quest for Beauty*. San Francisco and New York: W. W. Norton & Company, 1985.

Peck, Scott. *The Road Less Traveled, 25th Anniversary Edition: A New Psychology of Love, Traditional Values and Spiritual Growth*. New York: Touchstone, 2003.

Popcorn, Faith. *The Popcorn Report: Faith Popcorn on the Future of Your Company, Your World, Your Life*. New York: Harper Business, 1992.

Richo, David. *How to Be an Adult: A Handbook on Psychological and Spiritual Integration*. New York: Paulist Press, 1991.

Robbins, Anthony. *Awaken the Giant Within: How to Take Immediate Control of Your Mental, Emotional, Physical, and Financial Destiny!* New York: Free Press, 1992.

———. *Unlimited Power: The New Science of Personal Achievement*. New York: Free Press, 1997.

Roger, John, and Peter McWilliams. *Wealth 101: Getting What You Want, Enjoying What You've Got*. Los Angeles: Prelude Press, 1992.

Sarno, John, M.D. *Mind Over Back Pain: A Radically New Approach to the Diagnosis and Treatment of Back Pain*. New York: Berkeley Publishing Group, 1999.

Schuler, Robert H. *The Be Happy Attitudes: 8 Positive Attitudes that Can Transform Your Life*. New York: Bantam Books, 1987.

Scott, Dru. *How to Put More Time in Your Life*. New York: New American Library, 1988.

Seligman, Martin. *Learned Optimism: How to Change Your Mind & Your Life*. New York: PocketBooks, 1998.

Sher, Barbara, and Annie Gottlieb. *Wishcraft: How to Get What You Really Want*. New York: Ballantine Books, 1986.

Sinetar, Marsha. *Ordinary People as Monks and Mystics: Lifestyles for Self-Discovery*. New York: Paulist Press, 1986.

———. *Do What You Love, The Money Will Follow: Discovering Your Right Livelihood*. New York: DTP, 1989.

———. *Elegant Choices, Healing Choices*. New York: Paulist Press, 1989.

———. *Living Happily Ever After: Creating, Trust, Luck, and Joy*. New York: Villard Books, 1990.

———. *Developing a 21st-Century Mind*. New York: Villard Books, 1991.

———. *To Build the Life You Want, Create the Work You Love: The Spiritual Dimension of Entrepreneuring*. New York: St. Martin's Press, 1996.

Storr, Anthony. *Solitude: A Return to the Self*. New York: Ballantine Books, 1989.

Sun Tzu. *The Art of War*, trans. Samuel B. Griffith. Oxford, UK: Oxford University Press, 1971.

Taylor, Harold L. *Making Time Work for You*. New York: Dell Publishing, 1983.

Viorst, Judith. *Necessary Losses: The Loves, Illusions, Dependencies and Impossible Expectations That All of Us Have to Give Up in Order to Grow*. New York: Fireside, 1998.

Williams, Edward E., and Salvatore E. Manzo. *Business Planning for the Entrepreneur: How to Write and Execute a Business Plan*. New York: Van Nostrand Reinhold Company, 1983.

Zdenek, Marilee. *The Right-Brain Experience: An Intimate Program to Free the Powers of Your Imagination*, 2nd ed. New York: Two Roads Publishing, 1996.

about the author

Kenneth Atchity (B.A. Georgetown, Ph.D. Yale), "the story merchant," has authored books, screenplays, poems, short stories, articles, and reviews as well as produced films for television and theater. Since resigning from his tenured position as a professor of comparative literature at Occidental College, Ken has created his own Type C dream lifestyle around the work he loves the most: storytelling.

As a writer, literary manager, motion picture producer, and entrepreneur, he acquires, conceives, develops, and produces stories of his own and others through The Writer's Lifeline, Inc. (*www.thewriterslifeline.com*); manages through Atchity Entertainment International, Inc. (*www.aeionline.com*); and partners with companies like Warp & Weft (with John Scott Shepherd) and Originaliti Media, Inc. (with Sue Baechler an Garby Leon).

In AEI's first few years of operation, the company made $27 million in sales for first-time writers and produced *Joe Somebody*, directed by John Pasquin (*The Santa Clause*), starring Tim Allen and Jim Belushi; and *Life or Something Like It*, directed by Stephen Herek (*101 Dalmatians, Mr. Holland's Opus*), starring Angelina Jolie and Ed Burns; both based on scripts by John Scott Shepherd.

Ken's first study, as a teacher of literature, myth, dream, creative writing, and communications management, was focused on the continuum from dreaming to creative thinking to communicating to new realities (leading to his cofounding of the journal

Dreamworks: An Interdisciplinary Study of the Relationship between Dream and Art, published by Human Sciences Press from 1980 to 1986); and then to *A Writer's Time: A Guide to the Creative Process, from Vision through Revision* (W. W. Norton & Company). The recipient of grants and awards from the National Endowment for the Humanities, the National Endowment for the Arts, the Mellon Foundation, and the American Council of Learned Societies, he served as a Fulbright professor at the University of Bologna, teaching American literature and institutions.

Since his career transition, Ken's numerous films for television have included *Champagne for Two, The Rose Café, The Amityville Horror*, and *Shadow of Obsession*. AEI has managed literary and dramatic rights for *Ripley's Believe-It-or-Not!* and *The Learning Annex*. Ken served as writer and on-camera host for *Columbus: The Voyage of Discovery*, and has given lectures, seminars, and workshops for corporations and universities throughout the United States and Europe on aspects of myth, storytelling, Type C personality career transit, time- and mind-management, and creative thinking.

In addition to *Ripley's* and *The Learning Annex*, Ken's clients have included Steve Alten (*Meg, The Trench*), April Christofferson (*The Protocol, Patent to Kill*), professional poker player Sam Farha, financial analyst Kim Goodwin, Gary and Joy Lundberg (*I Don't Have to Make Everything All Better*), Shirley Palmer (*Lioness, Danger Zone*), Tracy Price-Thompson (*Chocolate Sangria, A Woman's Worth*), John Robert Marlow (*Nano*), James Michael Pratt (*The Last Valentine, The Lighthouse Keeper*), Governor Jesse Ventura (*I Ain't Got Time to Bleed, Do I Stand Alone?*).

He divides his time between New York and Los Angeles—as well as parts as far-flung as Manila, Vancouver, Rome, Rio de Janeiro and his native Louisiana.

contact the author

The author welcomes comments and questions, and can be reached at *jp@aeionline.com* or by snail mail:

c/o AEI
9601 Wilshire Boulevard, Box 1202
Beverly Hills CA 90210

For information regarding any phase of your writing career, visit *www.thestorymerchant.com* or contact The Writer's Lifeline at:

The Writer's Lifeline, Inc.
510 S. Fairfax Avenue
Los Angeles, CA 90036

Phone: (323) 932-0905
Fax: (323) 932-0905
E-mail: *amc@thewriterslifeline.com*

To receive the *Inspiration from the Story Merchant*, a free daily inspirational newsletter that includes events of importance to storytellers everywhere, email *inspire@thewriterslifeline.com*

Index

Books from Allworth Press

Allworth Press is an imprint of Allworth Communications, Inc. Selected titles are listed below.

The Money Mentor: A Tale of Finding Financial Freedom
by Tad Crawford (paperback, 6 × 9, 272 pages, $14.95)

The Secret Life of Money: How Money Can Be Food for the Soul
by Tad Crawford (paperback, 5 1/2 × 8 1/2, 304 pages, $14.95)

Your Living Trust and Estate Plan: How to Maximize Your Family's Assets and Protect Your Loved Ones, Third Edition
by Harvey J. Platt (paperback, 6 × 9, 336 pages, $16.95)

Estate Planning and Administration: How to Maximize Assets and Protect Loved Ones
by Edmund T. Fleming (paperback, 6 × 9, 272 pages, $14.95)

Old Money: The Mythology of Wealth in America
by Nelson W. Aldrich, Jr. (paperback, 6 × 9, 340 pages, $16.95)

Feng Shui and Money: A Nine-Week Program for Creating Wealth Using Ancient Principles and Techniques
by Eric Shaffert (paperback, 6 × 9, 240 pages, $16.95)

The Tragedy of Zionism: How Its Revolutionary Past Haunts Israeli Democracy
by Bernard Avishai (paperback, 6 × 9, 408 pages, $16.95)

Secrets of the Exodus: The Egyptian Origins of the Hebrew People
by Messod and Roger Sabbah (hardcover, 6 1/4 × 9 1/4, 304 pages, 175 b&w illus., $24.95)

Please write to request our free catalog. To order by credit card, call 1-800-491-2808 or send a check or money order to Allworth Press, 10 East 23rd Street, Suite 510, New York, NY 10010. Include $5 for shipping and handling for the first book ordered and $1 for each additional book. Ten dollars plus $1 for each additional book if ordering from Canada. New York State residents must add sales tax.

To see our complete catalog on the World Wide Web, or to order online, you can find us at ***www.heliospress.com.***